Onedia N. Gage

# The Blue Print

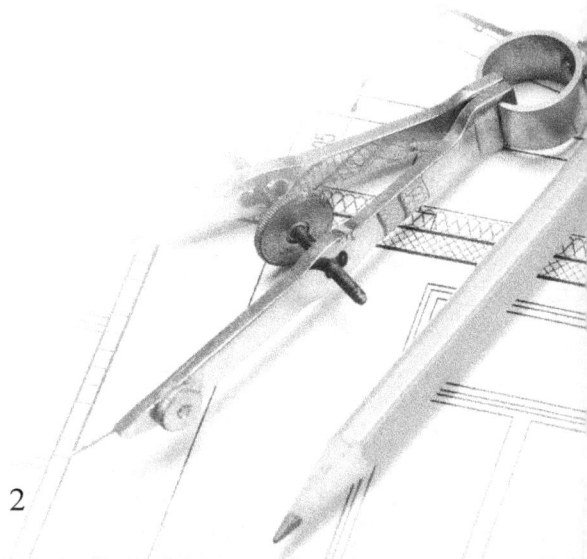

The Blue Print "Poetry for the Soul"

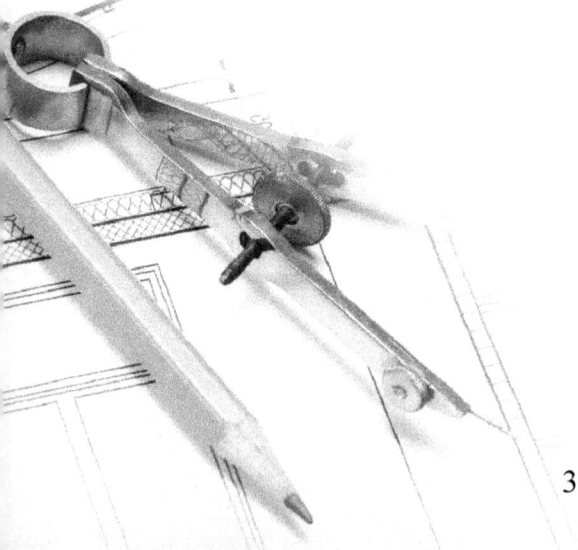

# The Blue Print

## "Poetry for the Soul"

### By

### Onedia N. Gage

The Blue Print "Poetry for the Soul"

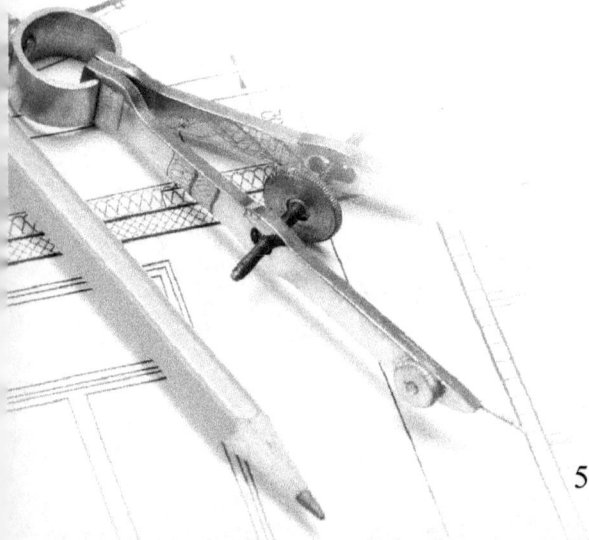

Consider it all joy, my brethren, when you encounter various trials.
James 1:2 (NAS)

I press toward the mark for the prize of the high calling of God in Christ Jesus.
Philippians 3:14 (KJV)

Be still and know that I am God.
Psalm 46:10

O Lord, Our Lord, how excellent is thy name in all the Earth!
Psalm 8:1 (KJV)

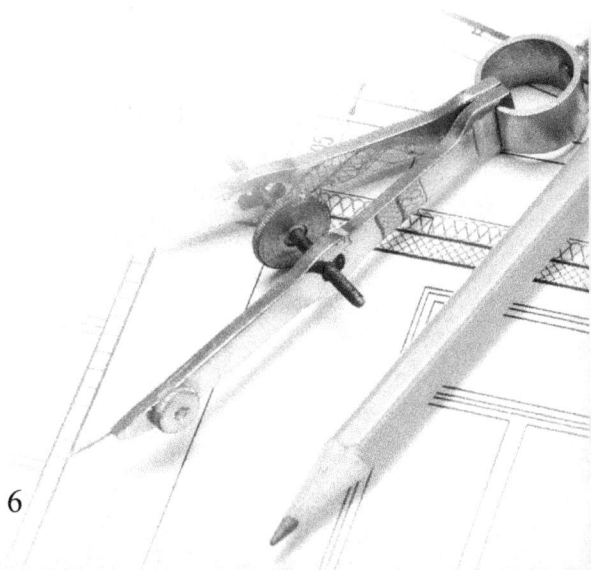

The Blue Print
Poetry for the Soul

All Rights Reserved © 2010 Onedia N. Gage

No part of this of book may be reproduced or transmitted in
Any form or by any means, graphic, electronic, or mechanical,
Including photocopying, recording, taping, or by any
Information storage or retrieval system, without the
Permission in writing from the publisher.

Purple Ink, Inc. Press

For More Information:
Purple Ink, Inc
P O Box 27242
Houston, TX 77227
www.purpleink.net

ISBN: 978-0-9801002-7-3

Printed in United States

# DEDICATION

To Hillary Nicole
and
Nehemiah Christian

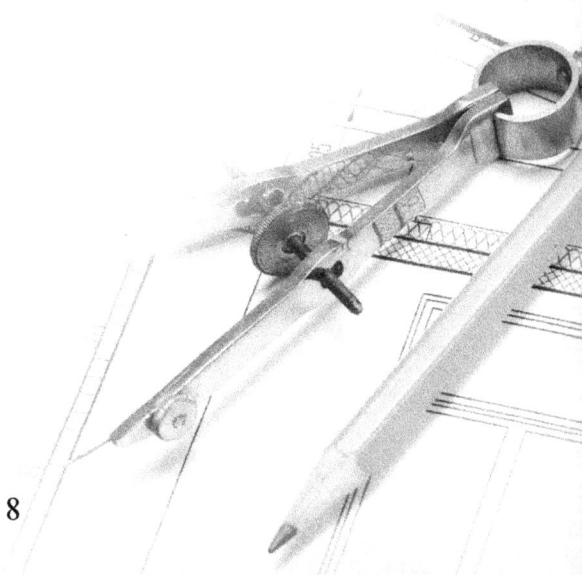

The Blue Print "Poetry for the Soul"

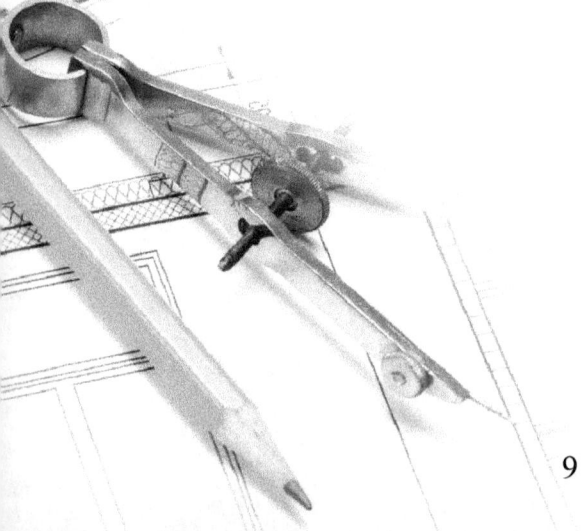

# ACKNOWLEDGEMENTS

To God, the Almighty, Omnipotent, Powerful Presence of Christ as You reside in my heart. Lord, I love You and I thank You for Your gifts and talents. I honor Your excellence and Your goodness. Teach me how to love you with my whole heart I adore you precious lord. You make my day bright when I'm alone; you make my burdens light.

God, thank You for Your plans for me. Thank You for **The Blue Print** and choosing me to complete Your project. I just want to please You. Thank You for continuing to anoint me and to invest in me and my gifts, which keep surprising me. Thank You for loving and forgiving me.

Hillary and Nehemiah, thank you for enduring my late nights, your ideas, the sounding board, the love and the support. Thank you for loving me, especially when I do nothing without a pen and a clipboard.

To my photographer, Ray Carrington, III. Thanks for making me look fabulous. Your photography is outstanding. Your creativity is truly wonderful. Thank you for your investment in my life.

To my graphic artist, Ron Nicholson and Picture Perfect Designs. Thanks for the art and imagination, for making my words look outstanding.

To my prayer partners and to my accountability partners, thank you for the long talks and the powerful prayers and the encouragement.

To the readers who this will reach and empower and touch and affect, may these words empower you and help you reach some resolve. May you be inspired to achieve your goals and dreams. May you enhance your relationship with God so that your other relationships will also improve. May you enhance your self-esteem through prayer and study. May you have courage and peace. Share love the best you can until you can share love without reservation.

Randy L. Boone: My Prayer Warrior intercedes. Thank you for each prayer on my behalf, in my place. God gives through people whose motives are pure and whose rights are relinquished. Randy, God has definitely given through you. Thanks to Shannon, Shanel and Shawna. Thank you for the title.

Special Thanks to Nikki Giovanni, .Alice Walker, Sonia Sanchez, and Maya Angelou.

To my church family: Pastor & Mrs. Ralph Douglas West, The Church Without Walls—Brookhollow staff, Mr. & Mrs. Willie Brown, Mr. & Mrs. Dempsey Wells, Jr., The Weakley Family, and the women and the youth of the Brook.

The Blue Print "Poetry for the Soul"

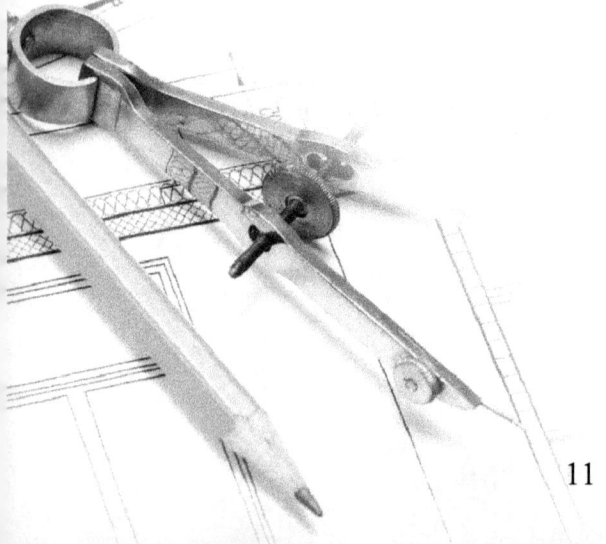

# JUST A NOTE

Dear Friend,

After you read several of these pages, only then will you know why I have been brief in my greeting. Everything I am and would want to say follows in these pages. This piece serves as my testimony for Philippians 4:13. "I can do all things through Christ which strengthens me."

May these words offer you peace and inspiration to achieve all the things for which you desire. Give with your whole heart to those things meaning the most to you. When you feel you're losing your way, stop and remember how far you've come.

If all else fails, continue to read these passages.

This is the ten year anniversary of this book. I hope it helps you as much as it has helped me over the years.

Love in purple,

*Onedia N. Gage*

Onedia N. Gage

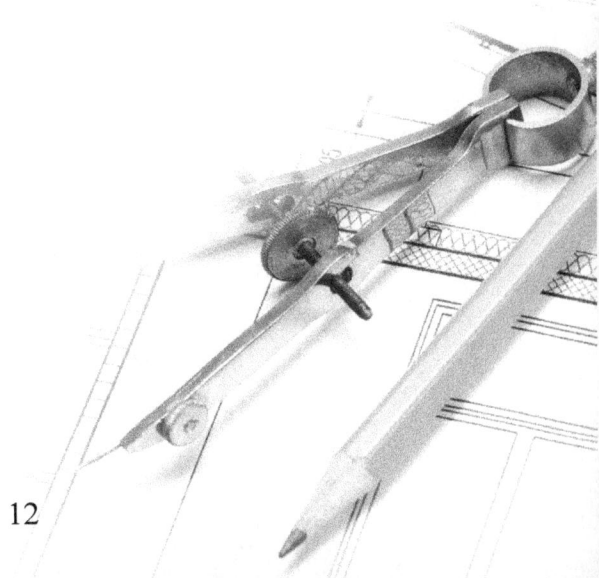

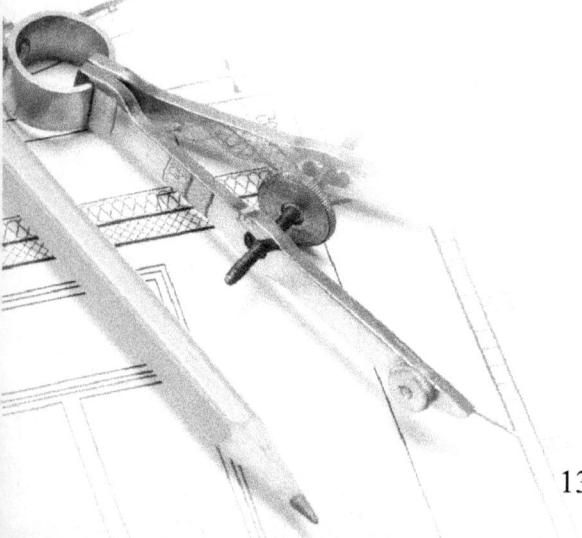

## TABLE OF CONTENTS

| | |
|---|---|
| Self Talk for Global Motivation | 18 |
| God's Higher Calling | 20 |
| Thoughts of You | 21 |
| Family: This Is For You | 22 |
| I Am for You | 23 |
| Looking at the World Through Rose Colored Glasses | 24 |
| And Who Created God? | 25 |
| I Almost Lost You | 26 |
| Only Me | 27 |
| Pray for Me | 28 |
| To Be Somebody | 29 |
| Roses and Best Friends | 30 |
| It's Been Too Long | 31 |
| An Affair of the Heart | 32 |
| Love | 33 |
| Better Days | 34 |
| Never as Good as the First Time | 35 |
| Loving Me | 36 |
| Going Away | 37 |
| Promises | 38 |
| The Dawn of Our Love | 39 |
| Life Long Longing | 40 |
| (Remember) | 41 |
| A Blossoming Romance | 42 |
| How Lonely is the Rain | 43 |
| (Be Patient) | 44 |
| Speaking on History | 45 |
| The Significant Other | 46 |
| Contemplation | 47 |
| Holding On | 48 |
| Reflection | 49 |
| Soul Mates | 50 |
| This Relationship | 51 |
| Best Friends | 52 |
| Fort Knox | 53 |
| One More Try | 54 |
| May 22, 1994 | 56 |
| Memory | 58 |
| An Artist At Work | 59 |
| The Gift | 60 |
| Revolutionary | 62 |
| Don't Know Me | 63 |
| The Battle Within | 64 |
| He Stands in You | 65 |
| All That I Have | 66 |

# TABLE OF CONTENTS

| | |
|---|---|
| She | 67 |
| The Man in Front of You | 68 |
| Wounded | 70 |
| Search | 72 |
| Exposure | 74 |
| Runaway | 76 |
| Tears | 77 |
| Defining Moments | 78 |
| The Tie that Binds | 79 |
| Life and Its Rewards | 81 |
| Don't Want to Rush, Don't Want to Wait | 82 |
| Not the Reverse | 84 |
| The Blueprint | 85 |
| Missing You | 86 |
| Issues | 87 |
| Power & Dominion | 88 |
| Small Talk | 89 |
| Oneness | 90 |
| Dear Architect | 92 |
| Middle | 93 |
| One Year | 94 |
| One Kiss | 96 |
| Those Deep Eyes | 98 |
| Wishful Thinking | 99 |
| Can You Promise? | 100 |
| Never Satisfied | 102 |
| A Dad's Love | 103 |
| The Handkerchief | 104 |
| The Price You've Paid | 105 |
| The Circle of Love | 106 |
| Perfect World | 107 |
| As One | 108 |
| For This Lifetime | 119 |
| Rain Drop Dreams | 110 |
| Love's Leadership | 111 |
| Artist's Eyes | 112 |
| Perfect Words | 113 |
| Miles of Flowers | 114 |
| Venus & Mars | 115 |
| Silly | 116 |
| She Walks | 118 |
| In Retrospect | 120 |
| The Glue | 121 |
| Dreamed | 122 |

Onedia N. Gage

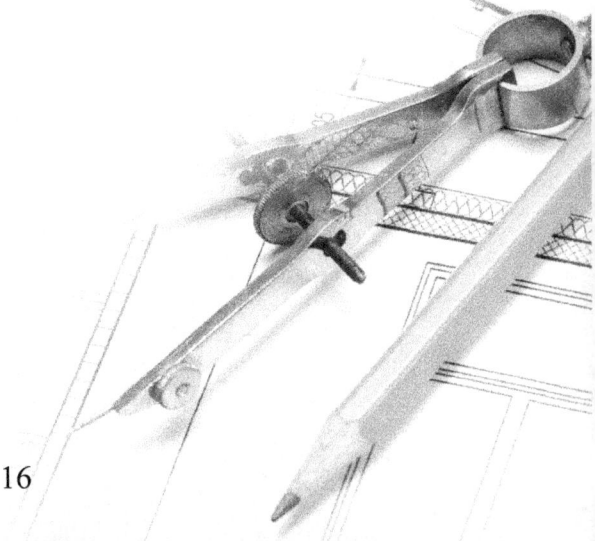

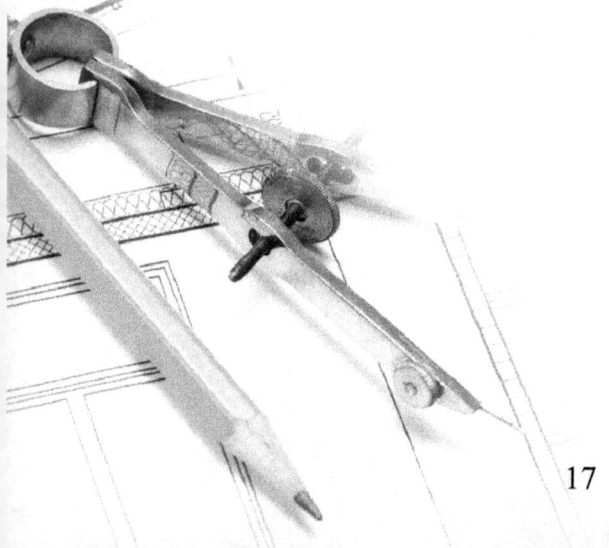

# SELF TALK FOR GLOBAL MOTIVATION

I believe in me because
in me there's a strength
that makes me strive for
ultimate success derived
from my goals because
there's a hope that I
will overcome my doubts and fears
that I have developed through failures
and rejections for which I have
decided are deficiencies in my character or/and
abilities when in fact those
mistakes stemmed from lack
of information (about that topic)
so after some education I have
made fewer mistakes and become
more intelligent so now I can draw
a new conclusion that
I have to love myself to love others
and I have to forgive myself before
I can forgive others and I have to respect
myself as an independent individual
before I can accept another person
and understand them and I know
I must learn before I can teach and
I have to fail before I succeed
and I need to see and understand before
I can show and share and I have to
be at peace with myself before
I can be at peace with the world
so now I know that believing in
me is true and real and necessary
to continue to radiate the strength
and power that my mind and
body and emotion encompass so that
I then believe in myself that I can
accomplish anything and everything
that I set out to do for myself,
my feminism and my people and my
brothers and sisters of color.

My belief is rooted in the faith
in myself to overcome barriers that
are set in front of me for the
betterment of myself and my counterparts

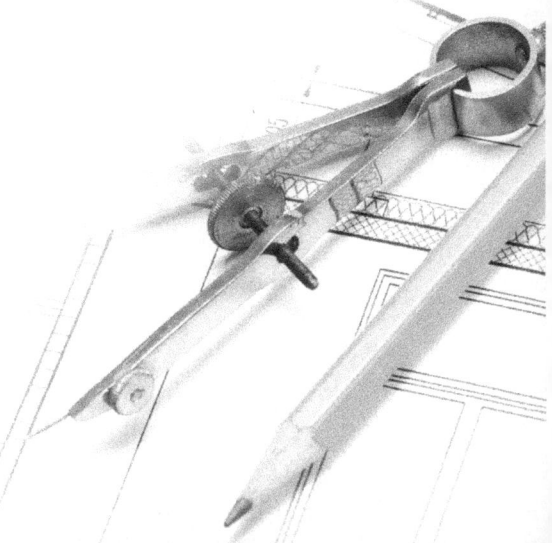

of color and this belief will create a
sense of motivation and inspiration that
I use as fuel for my soul and then
be able to transfer that power to
others to uplift them so that we
can all rise together for the enhancement
of us all so we can continue to
challenge ourselves to cultivate the
creative spirit that we all
share so that we can put those
deep souls and creative spirits and dedicated hearts
to work to make this aspiration operable for
our culture so that the world can
see that we are not ordinary
individuals but special
and extraordinary beings that have an
ultimate goal to be on top as the
majority of this world in numbers
and intelligence
for this is my and
our goal and we are going to
continue to strive for its success
because we are African American and therefore
determined.

      I live for this cause.

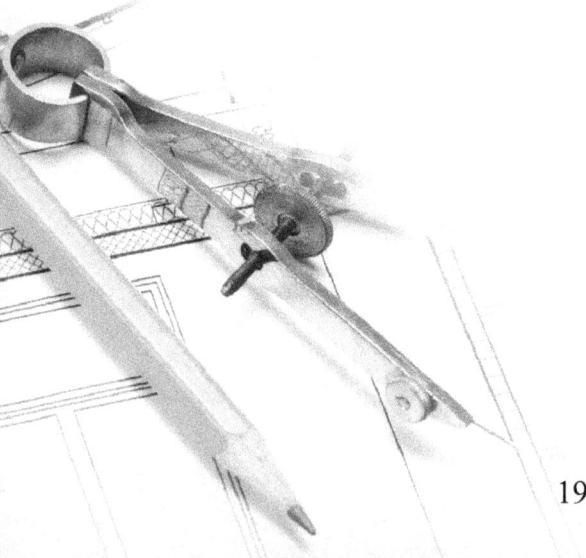

# GOD'S HIGHER CALLING

*"Oh Lord, Our Lord, how excellent is thy name in all the Earth." Psalm 8:1*

Lord, You have a higher calling for my life.
Lord, You have a divine plan for my being.
At Creation, Your will was to be done.

Lord, I want to be in Your will
Teach me Lord to walk in the steps of those of Jesus.

This higher calling of God's is hard to answer
Hard to comprehend
Harder to explain
Hardest to surrender

This Calling—Your will—is immeasurable yet dynamic.

This calling elevates me from the lustful desire
from the sinful nature
from the inexcusable activity
from the evil
from anything that inhibits my relationship with You, Christ

This calling demands my abundant giving
Compassionate spirit
Heartfelt love
At each moment of each day to ALL.

Lord, show me love and show me how to love
Lord, equip me to reach this calling
A calling where only You can receive the glory and the praise

Lord, heighten my spirituality to be the blessing You designed
Lord, You yearn for my obedience—make me yearn for my obedience

Lord, I Love You
I don't want to disappoint you
I don't want to miss nor misunderstand Your calling on my life

*"A godly woman who can find?" Proverbs 31:10*

God, I'm listening for the call.
    Your Higher Calling.

# THOUGHTS OF YOU

I listen to my music loudly in an attempt to drown my thoughts

Thoughts collective of dreams, goals, triumphs, failures, sunshine, rain, pain, fears, but mostly of love

Love to give and to give and to give but no one to receive

Receive with joy and thanksgiving, respect and reverence, appreciation and love

Love for the total person, person who will take extra care in the love and care

Care to take care of your feelings and fears; your goals and aspirations; your love and inspiration as my own.

Mutual inspiration that will transform into reality—love into a lifetime of fulfillment that replenishes the spirit and nurtures the soul

Soul, another, whole other one that will pair with yours to grow and caress,

Mate, companion . . .
    Best friend.

Friends that are lovers; lovers that are soul mates; soul mates that will spend a lifetime together as a passionate and a loving two through Him as we grows to Him, growing as one.

One that will last a lifetime

What God has joined, let no man put asunder.

Now I'm not sure why I try to drown out my thoughts.
Especially when mostly they are of you.

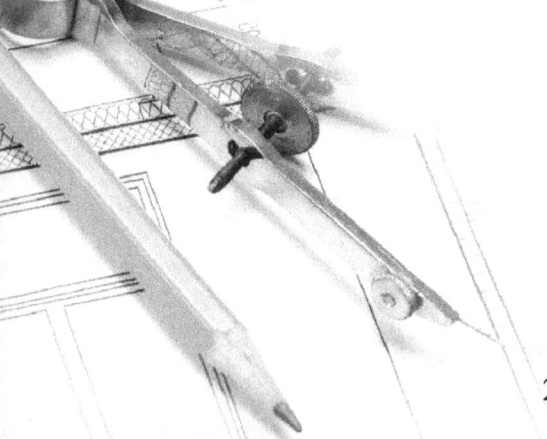

# FAMILY: THIS IS FOR YOU

I often feel that I cannot share
because I don't trust those that are there

When contemplating a problem or
some bright idea I have,
I think: "Will they hear me or
will my thoughts fall on deaf ear?"
More often than not I draw
within myself because I find the latter
to be true.

Lately, I've wanted to laugh with my
family but when I start to laugh
I stop because I wonder if instead of laughing
with me, they are laughing at me;
and lately it's been true.

When they are behind closed doors and I
hear murmurs, I ponder what all the talk
is about and upon viewing
of their faces, I am assured that
I am the topic of the conversation .

It's hard for me to put my feelings
into words for once shared,
I don't know what they will say.

However, I don't know what else to do;
there are only so many nights the lover
that I don't trust can rock me to sleep
and dry the tears that constantly fall.

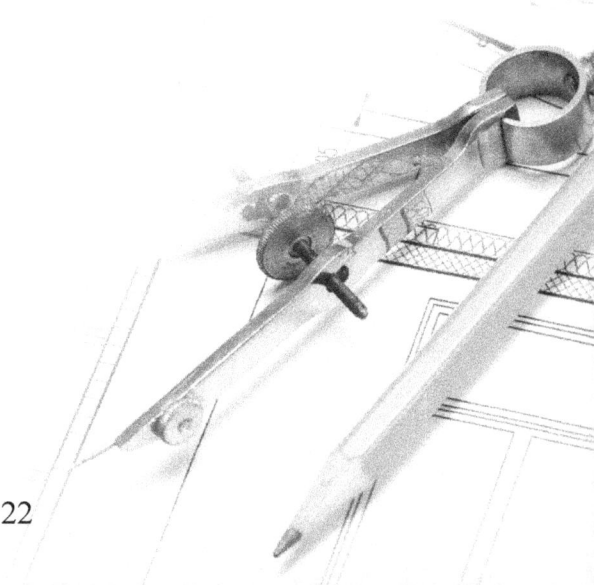

# I AM FOR YOU

The love I have
is buried deep within my soul
yearning to surface
desiring to respond
to tenderness and kindness

The love I have
is as pure as the silver lining
found inside a cloud
it storms and rages to show proof
of its innocence and sincerity
for you and your inner-self

I feel for you
I need your love and care
Your touch, your warmth
Your embrace; your hugs and kisses
to comfort and soothe
and support and confide
Me in you and you in me

For this love is an unrelinquishing love
One that burns deep into the night
Igniting the souls of truth into spirits
of emotional wealth

I want for the spirits that we harbor
to become one in feeling, emotion, and soul
for two loves that are destined
to become one shall be bonded in all
fashions to build the best
and most everlasting relationship

This I commit to thee because
you mean the world to me
My spirit would not be complete
without a bond with yours

Share with me your all,
I'll always be here for you
because I am for you.

# LOOKING at the WORLD THROUGH ROSE COLORED GLASSES

See, it's not like you think it is, not at all;
Let me explain:
I see things with a new style, a new "light";
People are little more tanned,
Sometimes bright and glowing,
Objects are a little different in color,
You see, vibrant purple calms to a baby's lavender,
Soft yellow turns to a bright peach.

I don't see things very clearly:
My colored vision gets blurry-the issues change upon inspection
They could be more appealing or more appalling-
It all depends on if I rolled into the blinds before I hopped out of bed

Sometimes this distorted perception of the world brings me trouble
But not for long
'Cause you see the effects go two ways:
I don't see out very well sometimes
But my advantage lies in my distraction it causes you
To understand the "me" behind the hint of rose
The real me is never displayed for the public:
It's shy and sensitive and caring and loving
But you'll never know proof of this because
I'm looking at the world through rose colored glasses
But this also means that you're looking through rose-colored glasses
To see me.

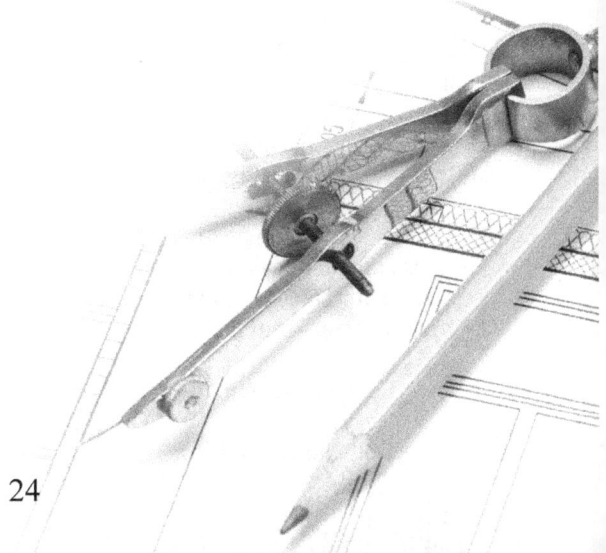

# AND WHO CREATED GOD?

Where did all of this come from--
The growth of the Earth,
This mush of ozone layer that deteriorates
As your eyes pass over this page

From where does Moses see the Creation
How did they become the Writers of the Books of Law
Who chose them as the twelve disciples

Who of them gave John the Baptist the
Humbleness, the honor, the privilege of
Placing Jesus under the waters of the Jordan

Who realized that Paul preached the
First Acts' sermon
And the generations and generations
Flow for days on end

How did we become Black--darker than
Everyone else--
I say that He made some in the day
And the rest at night.

"From whence cometh my help?" I ask.
They reply that thine help cometh from the Lord.
So when you say, "When did you see Him and how?"
They say have faith and keep praying.

This Lord that inspires, creates,
And destroys
He that hath made us and not we ourselves
From the clay and dirt and dust of this
Beautifully constructed Earth

He that controls our lives: emotions and actions.
He that loves for everlasting
And forgives forever
I love Him and I believe Him but
For those nonbelievers, from whence
I've heard and said all of the above to
This is your exact statement:

    So, God created all of this . . .

    But who created God?

# I ALMOST LOST YOU

We're holding each other close
Your concerns were mine &
My worries yours
Deeply connected to an everlasting bond-
A resource for understanding and compassion

Slowly you moved from me
I didn't bother to ask why
For only a microscope could notice
Surely you needed me
I waited patiently-
Not demanding-
Just hoping

I needed you to be strong for me
Stronger than I could ever be for you
However, I was misled
All the while, I held the power to
Rejuvenate but I was clueless.

Quietly you determined your escape only to fail
Your inner strength gathered and betrayed you blind
Your non-sustaining thoughts and hopes of departure
Left you surrounded by armed troops
The troops of love, faith, hope, happiness and forgiveness
Were being graciously guarded by many who desperately needed you . . .
ME!

You turned your back on me and refused to give me a chance to help
You shut me out and left me cold

You say that everything is fine
But will you ever really come back to me?

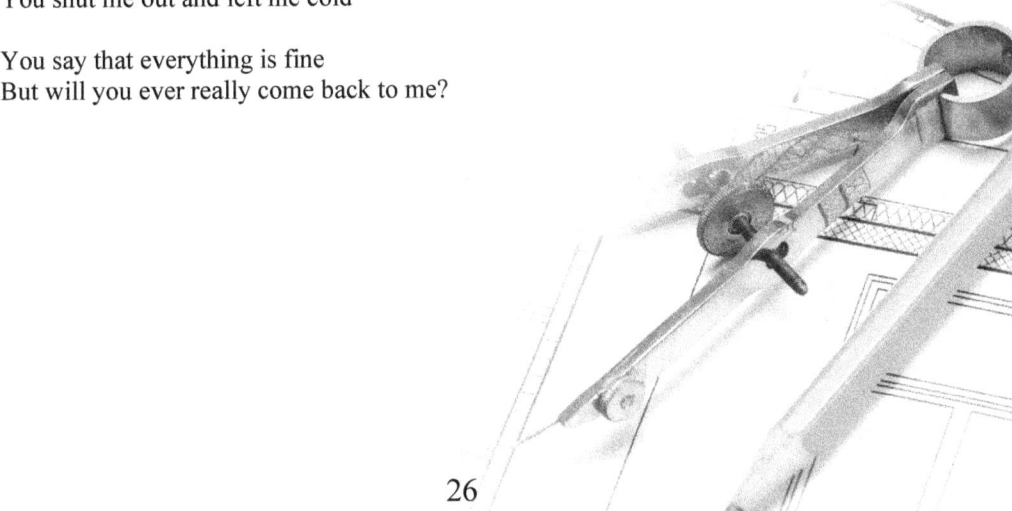

# ONLY ME

Shut out all the world
And hold me for a moment
Roll around and hold me
And leave the world outside

Treat them with a deaf ear
When I'm your first priority
Don't answer the phone
When you're next to me nude and warm

Shut down the calendars and schedules and meetings
And
        Love me and only me
        Hold me and only me
        Support me and only me
        Trust me and only me

For I'll be there for you when you need me and
It will be
        **Only me.**

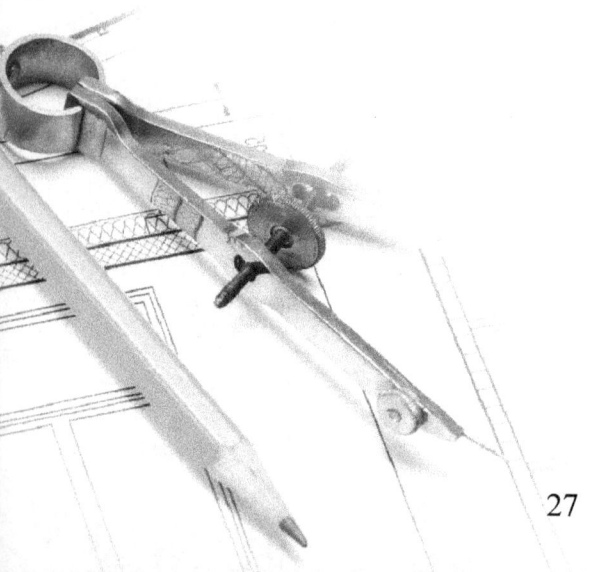

## PRAY FOR ME

Support me
When I have set goals for myself
So that I successfully accomplish them

See through me
When I'm untrue to myself
Set me straight
Show me the way

Provide me
With a means to seek knowledge
So that I can form educated opinions
And draw intelligent conclusions

Show me
Strength
So that I'll have support
If I should grow weak and restless
And I **will** grow weak and restless

But most importantly
Pray for me
For my morals
Strength
My perseverance and desire

Pray that I continue my pursuit of excellence
That I should never lose sight of my goals
That I remain persistent in my work
For these objectives and characteristics are important
And prayer is the most important of them all

Pray for me then I'll know that I won't fail.

# TO BE SOMEBODY

Old folks always said be somebody
and have something;
My grandmother once reminded me:

> to have something you have to be somebody
> to be somebody you have to have something
> to become somebody you have to have been
>     somebody anyway

so to be somebody and show thyself approved
as a "better" somebody
one must be determined to achieve
the highest mark possible
one must have decided for a stronger
being within themselves
one has to be supported and encouraged
to continue to strive for even their
remotest dreams
please don't forget to believe in yourself
and to love yourself
have faith
your biggest fans are God and self
always remind yourself that when
you reach your goals that there are
always other things to hope and dream for
so don't ever stop living to improve yourself
Also give it back to the community,
race and culture; all of it: love, support,
help, all of it to help those that don't have
any inspiration or self-motivation.

Give it back ten-fold.

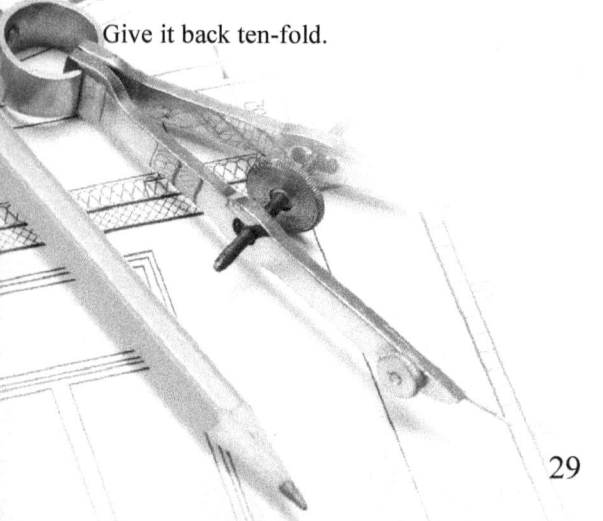

## ROSES AND BEST FRIENDS

A rose is just a rose
You don't have to describe it to anyone
A rose is a rose
You don't have to say how pretty it was
Or what color it is or how many you received
Cause when you say to your very best friend that
That special someone gave you a rose
She'll know exactly how you felt when you got it
She can imagine the look on your face
She'll ask did you scream but she'll know that
He said he loved you
She'll know how special the moment was
And how long you held it close
Because by being your best friend
She knows everything about you
That's what is special about roses and best friends:
They know how to make you feel special and
They are special, too.

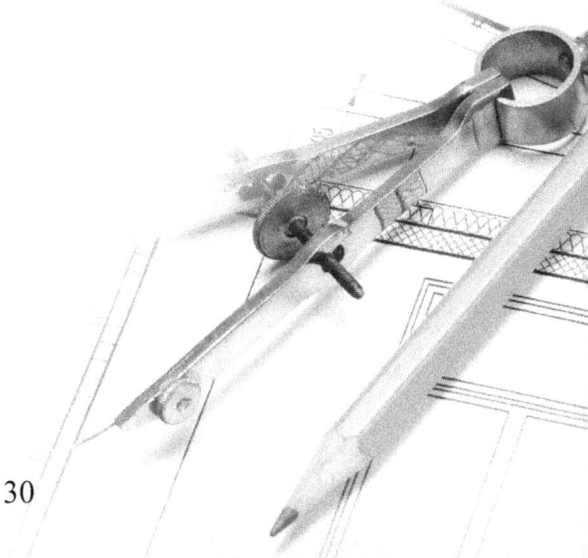

## IT'S BEEN TOO LONG

Holding you lifts my heart to the roof of the world
Kissing the stars is the excitement
I feel when I kiss your tender lips
Easing into a bed of motion near you
Makes me shake and shiver with passion
Touching and feeling and caressing makes my blood boil beyond control
My nerves escalate with the tension of my longing

What do I have to do to get my point over to you?

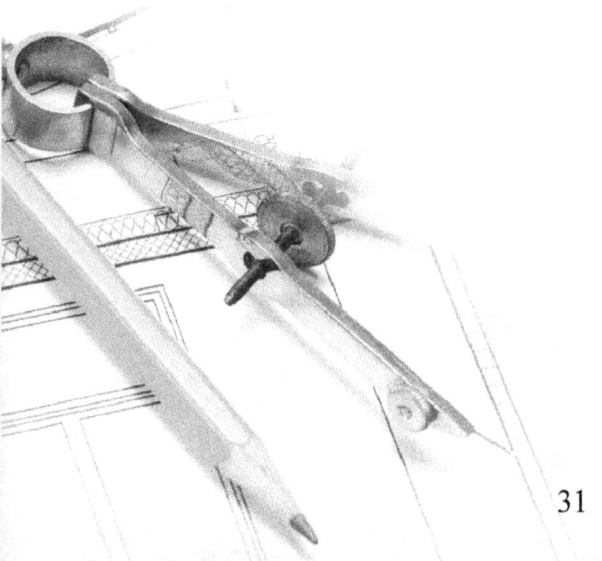

## AN AFFAIR OF THE HEART

You came like a thief in the heat of the night
You got my attention
You fulfilled my dreams
You gave me everything I asked for
Then like a thief, you took it all back.

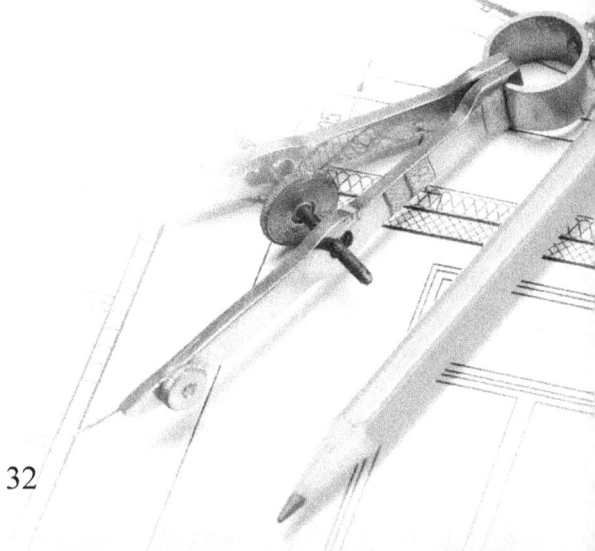

# LOVE

My first love is you
So special and warm
Strong and everlasting
Our hearts have grown together as one

Love as special as this one has to be
An endless love
You mean the world to me
I'll never let you go.

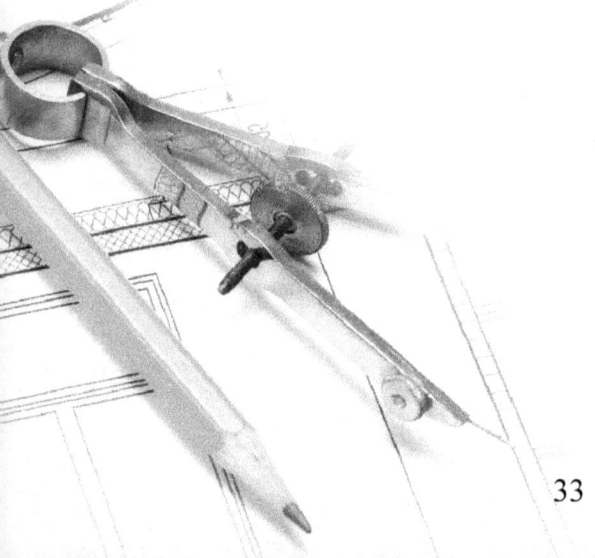

## BETTER DAYS

More sticky than peach preserves
More delicate than the finest china
More intense than the deepest hue
All above describes my love for you
I've shown my love for you
In all the ways I can
All others will come in later days
And in better ways.

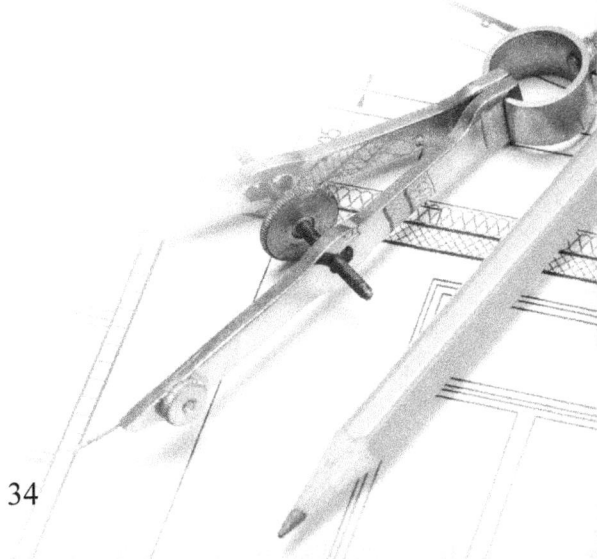

## NEVER AS GOOD AS THE FIRST TIME

If I were to kiss you and fall deeply in love with you again, tomorrow;
If I could make love to you at this very moment;
It'll never be as good as the first time.

If I should decide to renew our relationship
Try as I might to make it right
The deep love, the miraculous joy
That we once shared is gone
And it'll never be as good as the first time.

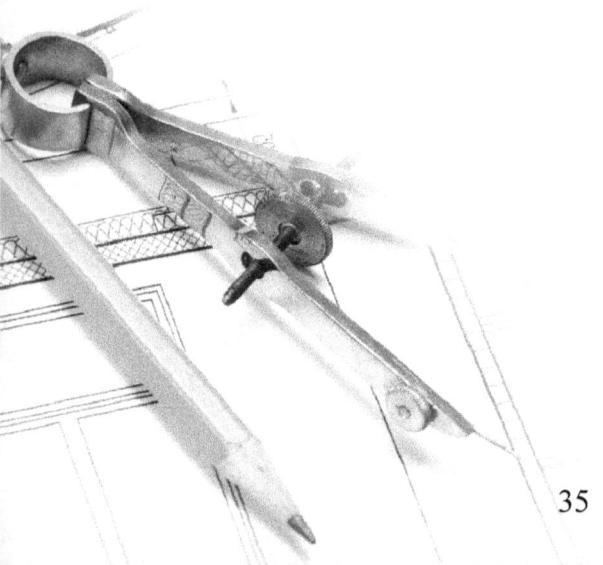

## LOVING ME

Inspire me & be inspired
Encourage me & be encouraged
Support me & be supported
Romance me & be romanced
Embrace me & be embraced
Love me & be loved

That's the solution to successfully loving me.

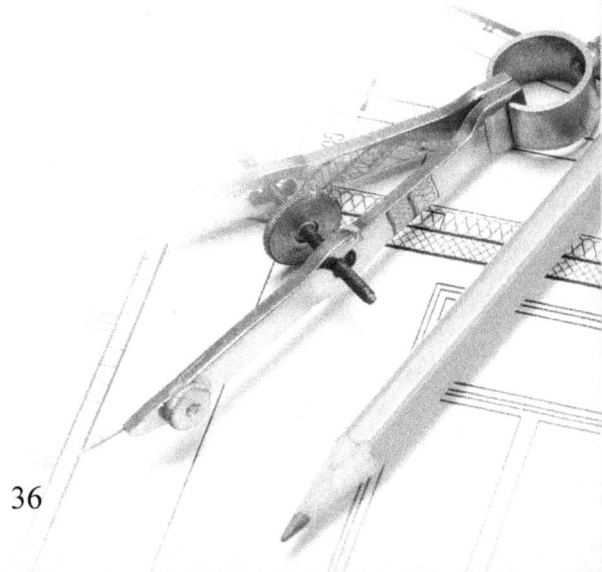

## GOING AWAY

You've walked into my life with no regrets
You've filled my heart with hopes and dreams and happiness
You've shown me true love but
You'll be leaving soon
Sooner than I want to admit to.

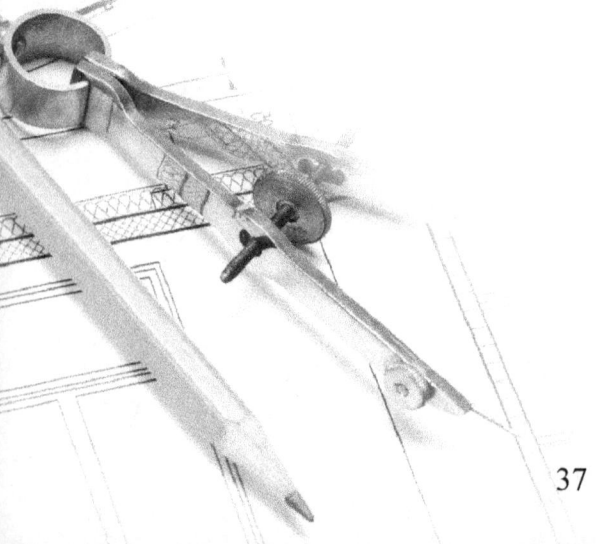

## PROMISES

I see you through the silver reflection of the rain
The sparkle of the drops remind me of the glow in your eyes
I'd pull out the silver lining of any cloud
If I thought it would make you happy
If I thought it would make our love last forever and ever.

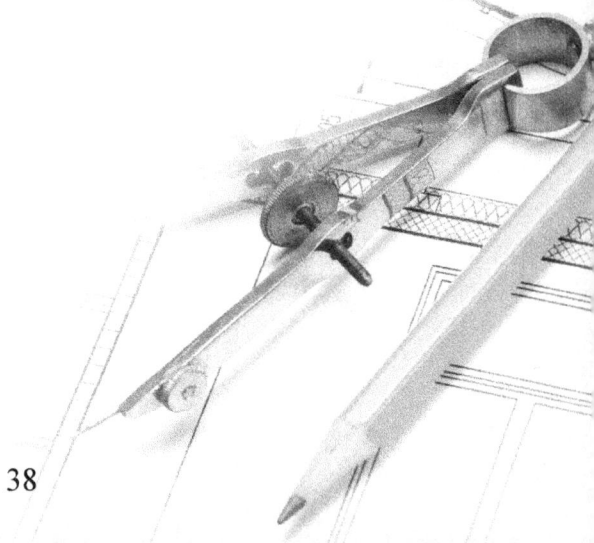

# THE DAWN OF OUR LOVE

Crisp cool spring breeze
Ocean waves splashing on the rocks
Sweet-salty smell of fresh salty sand
Brisk walk in the mellow atmosphere
Light pillowy air
Slow hazy sun rising in the hazy horizon

She cherishes the moment
Early morning rising
Inhale the light salty air
Feel the crisp springy breeze
In the early morning dew
Walking in the moments of love
On the damp-dewy sand
The light pillowy air caresses her slender shoulders
The coolness of the water alerts her senses
She becomes aggressive with the day
As slow and lazy as the sun rising in the horizon

He finally awakes; aware of her absence
He appears on the terrace searching the new morning
For signs of his lost companion
He spots her then joins her in the cool springy breeze

As the sun completely rises
So does the dawn of our love.

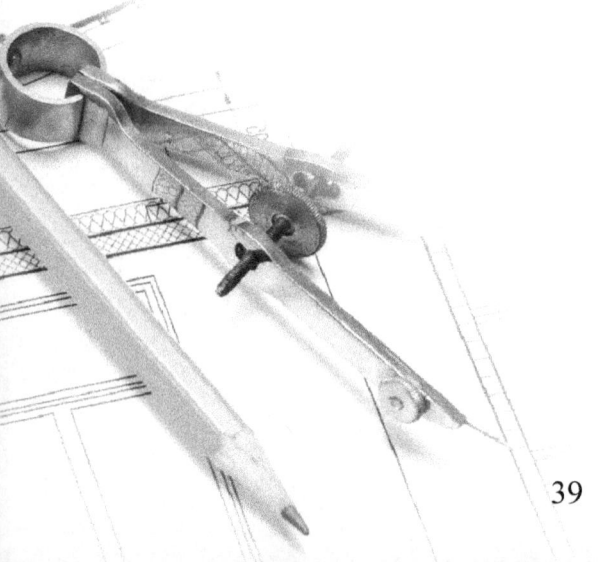

# LIFE LONG LONGING

He speaks with thoughts unheard
*He needs to be loved*

He wants a love with a match of his emotional intensity
*He expresses true emotions*

He wishes his feelings to be matched
*He longs to share his life*

His hopes and dreams are clear
*He pleads to be desired*

He requests the presence of an intellect with a caring soul
*His passion is a rushing, explosive river waiting to overflow*

He says with depth, he intends to love
*He needs to have someone to hold*

He pleads for someone with which to grow old
*He wants someone he can love bold*

**He ask for my love.**

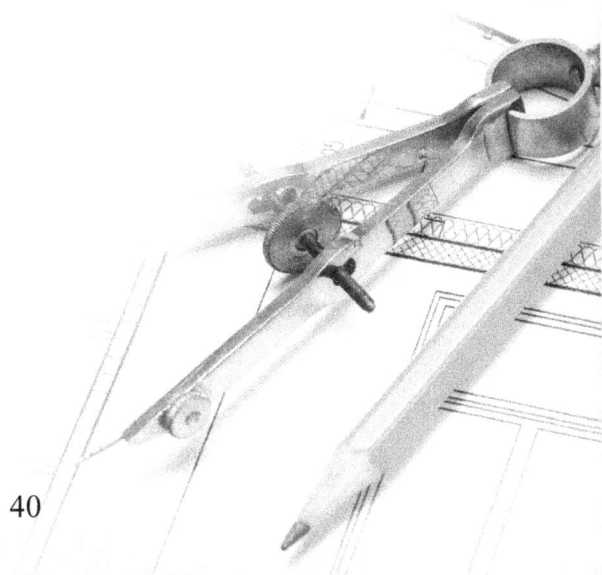

## (REMEMBER)

One doesn't fully appreciate
the sunshine until a few drops
of rain have fallen

Sunshine turns darkness into light,
however dark, one assumes that
light will come and soon

Make no assumptions of a positive
future, instead work diligently for your
sunshine

You can only achieve what you
set out to accomplish--without
effort, you can expect to receive nothing

You should love with no reservations
nor convictions, for a true love is
lasting love

You should appreciate a love
because once it's gone--you may
never see it again

Remember, one doesn't appreciate a true love until
it is no longer true.

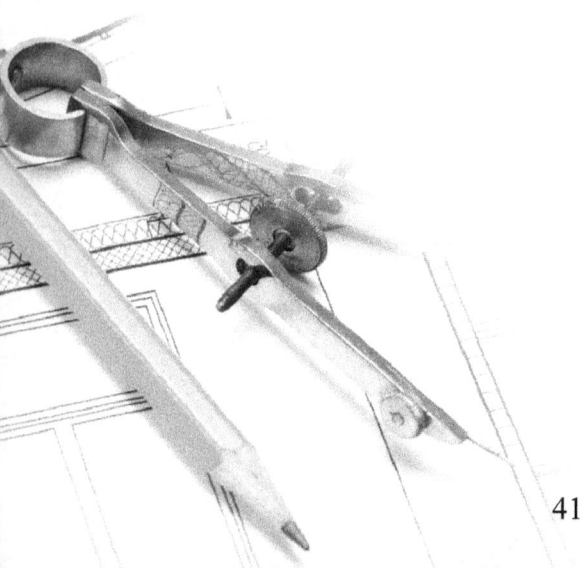

## A BLOSSOMING ROMANCE

Light conversation
easy listening
comfortable setting
dim lights
obvious attraction
Crown Royal
jazz whispers
sounds of the sea
Kendall Jackson
poetry
loose apparel
intimate glances
waterbed
frosted flakes
a dozen roses
silent commitment
and
imaginary mistletoe kissing

Could anything be better than a blossoming romance
at the end of a hot and humid winter?

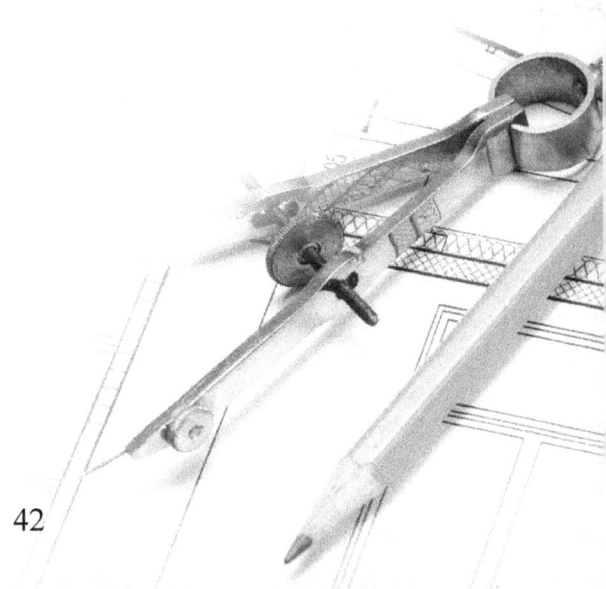

# HOW LONELY IS THE RAIN

How lonely the rain must be
When it comes out; it's all alone
No one to play with
No one to share with.
It appears first as slow as tears and
Everyone goes away.
"Rain, rain go away; come back some other day,"
They say, when they really don't mean that at all.
Don't people know that the rain wants
Love and companionship, too.
How lonely the rain must be
When it really finds one to love
And the lover leaves to find another home.
The heartbreak and pain insurmountable.
Oh my, the Rain.

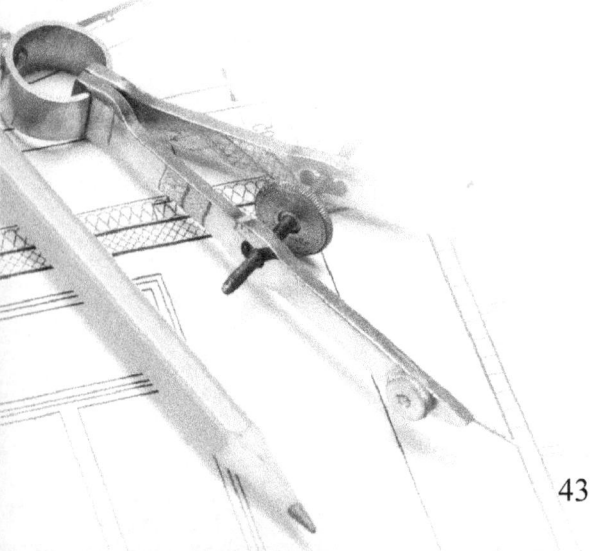

## (Be Patient)

My love for you has not faded away
It only grows stronger each day.
And as I stand here thinking of how to
Reopen my heart
The desire in your eyes made a healthy start.
Knowing that you love me
Encourages me each day, it
Explains my growing love for you
In every way.
So as I sit and continue to think
I realize that your love is real.
For if it had not been how could you stay
Around waiting and debating with me
About what exactly went wrong.
I used to doubt your love for me
But now I honestly feel it in my heart.
Thanks for your patient love.

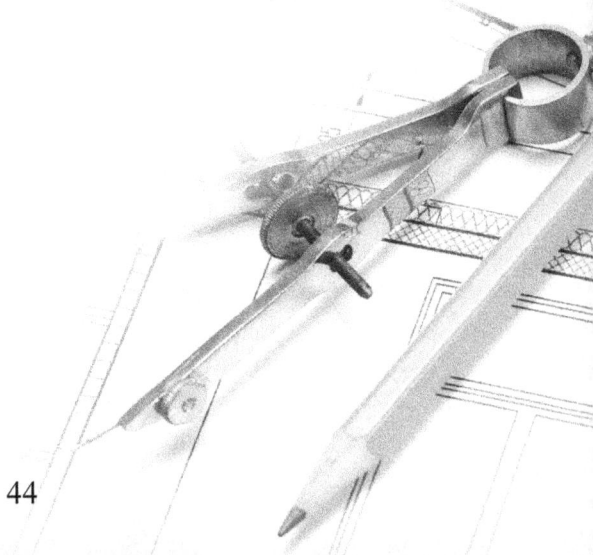

## SPEAKING ON HISTORY

We are a tired people
We only want to exercise, without restraint, the rights and privileges that are guaranteed by the bonds of this nation:
The Constitution of the United States
We no longer want to be denied the opportunity to express ourselves, not to become independent individuals when we desire
We need assurance of the acceptance that the world claims to have for us as humans, as people
Grant us those inalienable rights that we were born with -- we will work with you
So loose those shackles
Cut loose those chains
Destroy your prejudices and we'll teach you to love
We are human, too,
We are a people--
**We are a tired people!**

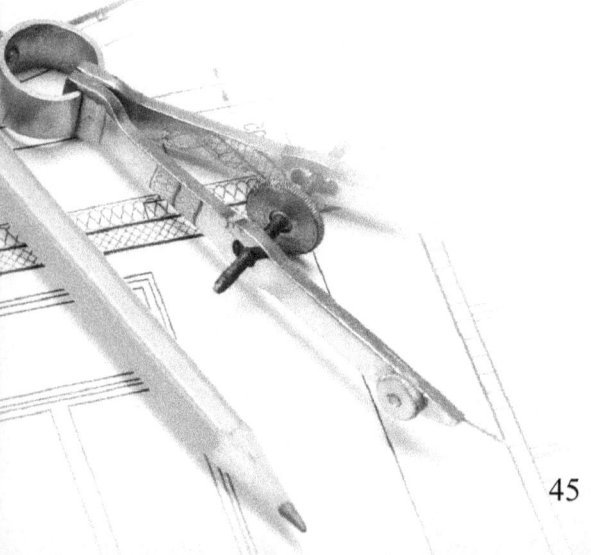

# THE SIGNIFICANT OTHER

One to have and to hold--
        to love, to cherish,
Only death will this diminish.
Forever will hold the two.
Because a real love is a forgiving love,
It doesn't assume nor deny anything.
The two respond openly, freely,
Communicate passion and care,
Desire the other's happiness and genuine satisfaction.
Love and be loved.
Live and let live.
Appreciate the beauty of the moments that the two share.
Romance the other person's favorite color
To the surface of their complexion.
Assure and reassure the depths of a responsive love.
Remind that "one" that the sun rises and sets within their eyes.
Remind them that they are
        The "Significant Other,"
           that you will not forsake them for some other.

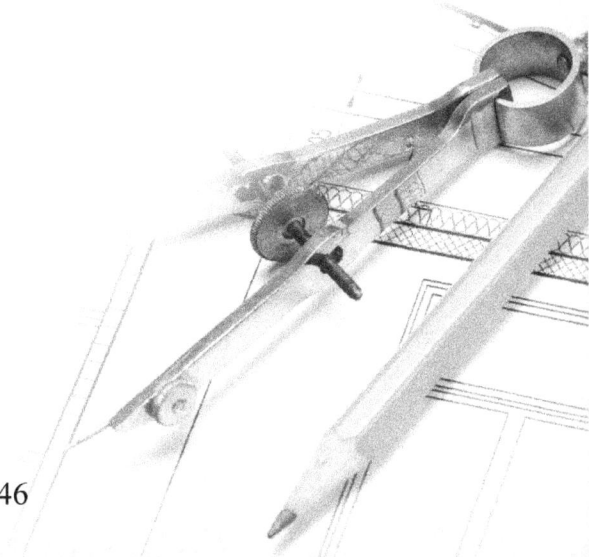

# CONTEMPLATION

Deep in thought
of the many wonders
that have been revealed to me
My mind has enjoyed
Many thoughts of you
Realizing the joys you bring to my heart.
Silently speculating on when I'll escort you into
My unconquerable soul.

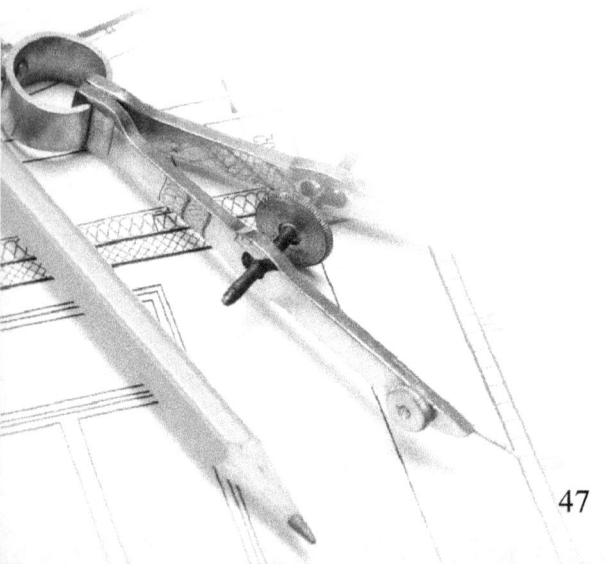

# HOLDING ON

I've been through four TV guides out of boredom

I've flipped through 100 channels for lack of anything to do

I've shed rivers of tears over problems that don't belong to me

My trials and problems and pains are many

My love and heart have held me and supported me

My soul is weary and weak

With my spirit and strength about to leave, I went to see my Lord today.

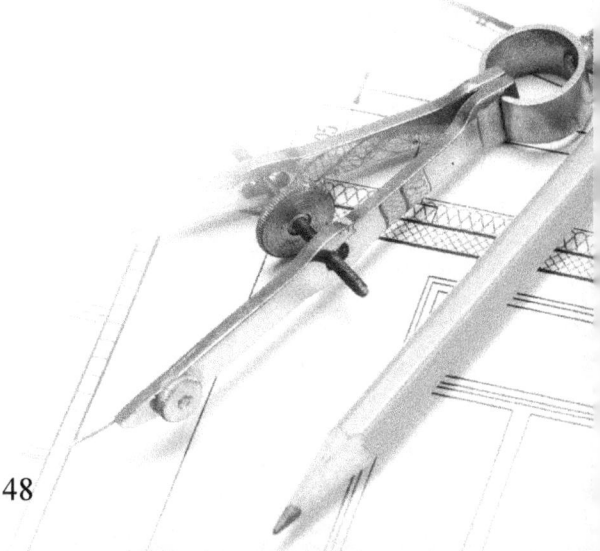

## REFLECTION

The day you say goodbye
Is the day that you see me cry
But don't fear because the first tear
You see is because I love you
Each tear after that tells of my hurt,
Unhappiness and memories of the time we've shared.

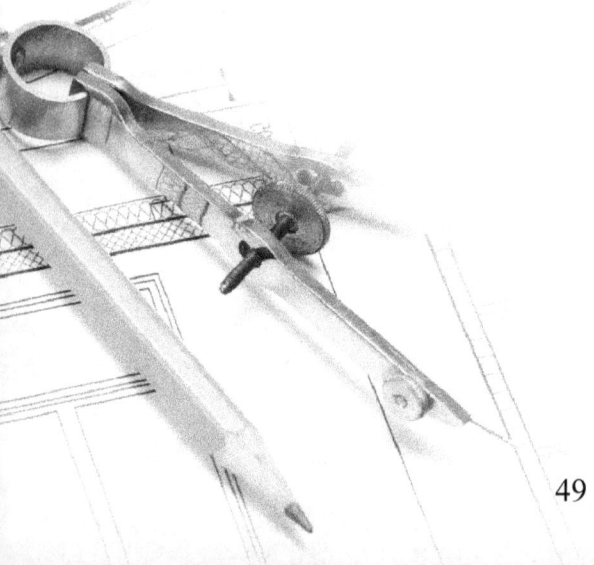

## SOUL MATES

I only want one part of you and that's your soul

Shower me with your thoughts, your fears, your dreams, your expectations, your disappointments

Your love will come - that's not my concern

You need someone to love, encourage, trust, support, and care for you

The window of your soul can be painted purple with my affection and love.

Don't laugh; Purple is my favorite color. Just imagine your soul's window shaded purple inviting me to care for it, love it, stroke it, cater to it, and fill it with my love, strength, power, sensitivity, respect, trust, forgiveness, selfless deeds, giving heart and receptive soul.

For my favorite color, I'll do it all. Purple is profoundly powerful, passionate, persuasive, peaceful, regal and religious.

I am all those things and so are you
Imagine our souls together:
All the things that I am with all
the things that you are . . .

All the things that we are not will become things that we can become together because of each other.

Soul Mates.

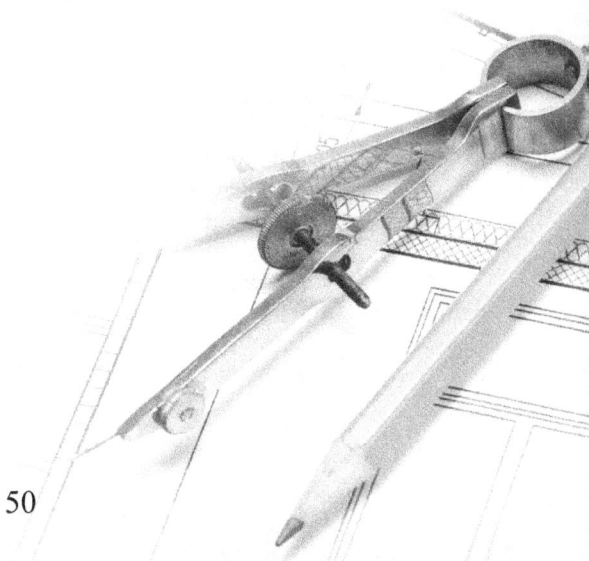

## THIS RELATIONSHIP

I guess maybe I'm unreasonable or surely I'm not living in reality because there is definitely something wrong.

This partnership has me yielding the most and profiting the least.

You deny the simplest request, yet I await your most complicated demand.

Is there anything that I could ask for that would soothe my soul and comfort my heart that wouldn't possibly inconvenience you so?

I guess realizing that I have needs and wants as you do was a surprise for you because fulfilling them has become quite a task for you.

You deny the simplest pleasures involved in creating and maintaining my happiness.

Are my expectations too many?
Are my wants too much?
Are my needs too taxing?
Are my burdens too heavy?

What do I need a relationship for if I'm not profiting and furthermore, I'm the only one not profiting from it?

Silly thoughts cloud my sanity, such as should we leave this relationship right here? Should we stop trying to make each other happy and start satisfying ourselves? Why has my reasoning become clouded by this thing called love?

My judgment is weak. Do you realize the effect that you've had on my mind? Do you realize the impact that you have made on my soul? Could I leave you without committing suicide of the heart, mind, body and spirit?

Is time apart the answer to all of these questions? Do I need space to sort these things out? Will that be profitable for me? For us?

There I go again, taking us into consideration. Maybe if every now and then I did what I damned well pleased then maybe I wouldn't be unhappy. Maybe I could refuse my significant other something of importance from me to him.

Would that be fair? Would you be hurt? On the other hand, it probably wouldn't bother you at all, or would it cut your emotions up into tiny pieces, too?

But then again why bother; all of it will probably be a waste of love.

# BEST FRIENDS

While walking along the beach
with my best friend, I confessed that
I wanted to get married some day.
He seemed surprised.

I told him that I had to love him,
honor him, cherish him and he me:
Love and be loved
live and let live
Cherish and sacrifice
Only death will this diminish
Forever will hold the two
Because a real love is a forgiving love.

As I spoke, I noticed a change in my friend.
He started slowly and thoughtfully about his
need for a giving lover and a caring mother.
For the future of his life includes a mother and a wife;
That she would be the moon and the stars.
And although cliché, she would forsake him for none other.
This spiritual being would insist on the best for him by
Demanding the only best from him.

We agreed that this search is not easy.
We promised to keep looking until we found the ideal mate:
A lifelong mate
that will assure and reassure
the depths of a responsive love
and will communicate passion and trust.
This mate will also be a friend.

Then without fear nor reservation, my best friend asked me to be his lifelong mate.
With bright eyes, I agreed
Then we knew the journey had just begun.

Today, I married my very best friend.

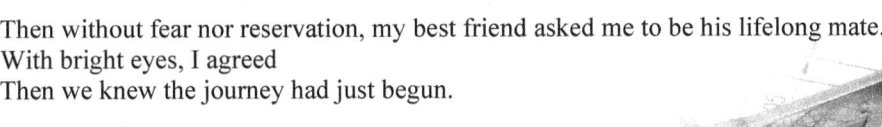

## UNLOCK FORT KNOX! – UNLOCK FORT KNOX!

Not the Fort Knox with the gold; I want into the Fort Knox that has your mind, heart, spirit, soul and all the other intimate faculties on strict security.

I want to enter your warm and forgiving soul because it is there where I'll find your strength.

I demand admittance into your perceptive mind because it is there where I'll see your power.

I have inquired several times about admittance to your heart because it is there where I'll encounter the buttons which trigger your smiles, your tears, your happiness, your pain.

I want in so that passionate and unyielding souls become one deserving one another. Yearning one another. Yielding to one another.

Conversations will become intimate rather than superficial.

I'm on a need to know basis and right now I need to know that the pain you feel can be shared through conversation:        a sentence, a word, a kiss, a hug, a touch, or as simple as a glance.
            Your joys and triumphs, too.

I know that it's hard to unlock Fort Knox for me
I'm not worried about falling in love though
I'm simply concerned about completing that love

I want the passion that I want, when I want it, from whom I want, and quite frankly, it's only you.

This may not be my final request, however it is the most profound by far.

I promise to handle it with extreme care and caution for the package is marked fragile.

I promise to give more than I receive.

I promise comfort, care, love, intimacy, passion, and total respect for our sharing.

I promise to keep your secrets secret.

I'd like to love you but I need your help. I can be trusted with it all.

"Hunger can see when satisfied can't."
Help me satisfy my hunger.

## ONE MORE TRY

You were once a stranger to me
But once I looked through your eyes
Into the window of your soul
I knew that you were the one
For me.

You say that you need me
Yet you are to leave me
The best teacher I've ever had
Is now about to leave me
All alone in this big cold world--
Take at least one more chance to
Try to keep our promises.

Alone without your love
I wonder if I will survive
I feel lost and I miss deeply
The warm security of your care
Try once more to fulfill our love.

I was to learn to love you
And hold you and feel you but I
Guess it's best I don't know 'cause
Now that you're leaving me, I'll
Have less to miss of you.

We need to try once more before
Throwing our love away for it is
Said that one doesn't miss what one
Has until it's gone. So the question
Is once the love is lost and gone
Away, can it be recovered? Or better
Yet should it be recovered?

For another moment you must try
To catch me before I fall--I've
Loved you to the fullest for the
Fullest is all I can give but if
It's rejection I continue to receive
It's probably best that you leave.
'Cause only so long will I grieve
For the best of your love.

I'm confused about the depth of your love

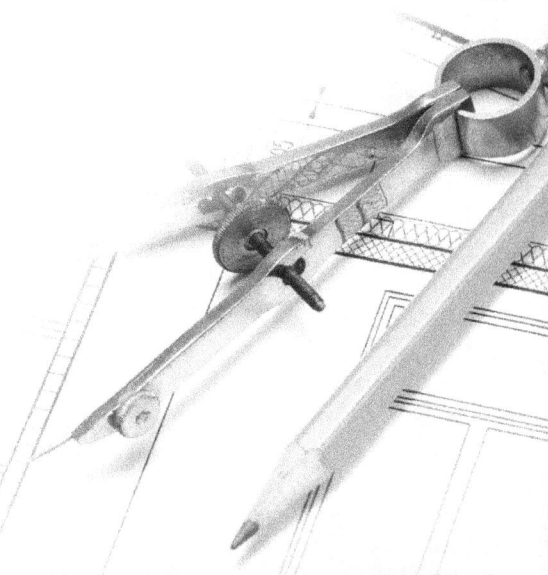

The strength of your commitment
I'm not sure what you meant
'Cause you said that you needed time
Away from my love
I've been suffering since your first
Departure and just when I regain the faith
In your love, you leave again.

So if you decide to leave me forever,
Make me believe you
Don't let me hope for things that
Will never be
Keep me away from the dangers
Of being hurt in case you don't
Return.

But please just one more try for
Love that feels lost and forgotten
For I love you more than you
Could ever know--
Don't ever forget that.

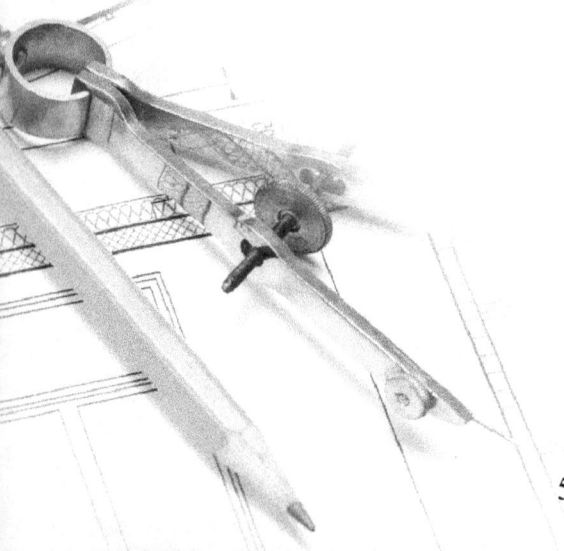

Onedia N. Gage

## May 22, 1994

This view takes me back to the days of old:

Before rap was vogue,
After Lady Heroin lost her following;

Before jazz became an indication of sophistication,
After peace could only be achieved through music;

Before soulstice.


Was it like this back
        when or then?

Was this how it felt to sit and
        watch Billie sing the blues?
            **--refreshed, excited--**

            Did Louis do trumpet solos into a microphone
                with simply his groove clothes on?
                **--inspired, thrilled--**

            How did the audience contain itself when
                Miles blew those notes as easily as a
            whisper?
                    **--content, elated--**

            Why did Coltrane choose down home jam sessions
                to express thoughts of self and others?
            **--confident, thoughtful--**


            What would the criterion be for the choice
                to do the *jazz* thing?

                      intimate        cozy
                      twilight        relaxed
            romantic    mellow
            untainted              majestic
            realistic     memorable


Mahogany brings the tears;
Brass brings the shivers;

Black and White offers the irrefutable comfort
    --**<u>soulstice</u>**


*these blues could make you loose your mind*
*or maybe even regain your senses;*

*for blues is the truth*
*truth is love*
*love those times*


Where would you find comfort to hear *that* best jazz thing?

        *downtown, Houston:  Soulstice*


"share the atmosphere"
"wallow in the ambiance"


feel the jazz
seek the comfort
discover the spirit


EXPERIENCE . . .

        **SOULSTICE.**

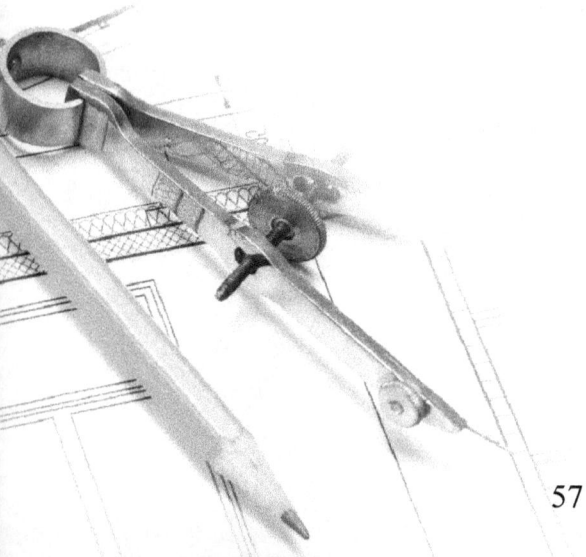

# MEMORY

My name, and my place, and my tomb all forgotten,
The brief race of time well and patiently run,
So let me pass away, peacefully, silently
Only remembered by what I have done.

Remember me when I am gone away,
Gone far away into the silent land;
When you can no more hold me by the hand,
Nor I half turn to go yet turning stay.
Remember me when no more,
Day by day,
You tell me of our future that you have planned;
Only remember me;
You understand it will be late to counsel then or play.

Yet if you should forget me for a while
And afterwards remember, do not grieve;
For if the darkness and corruption leave
A vestige of the thoughts that once I had,
Better by far you should forget and smile
Than that you should remember and be sad.

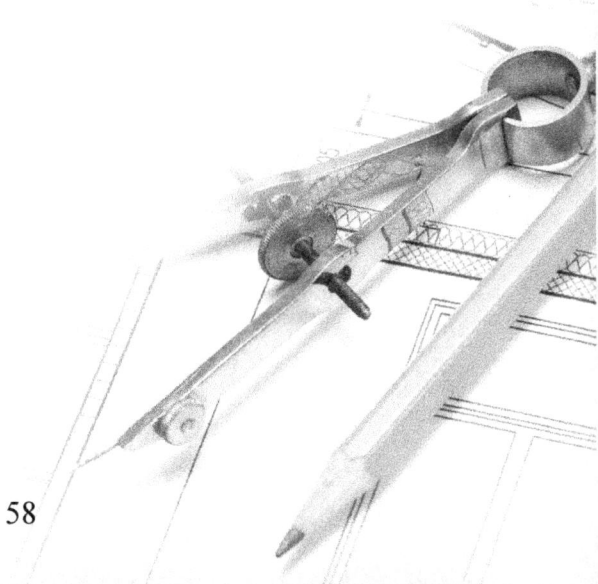

## AN ARTIST AT WORK

It's best to take art when you're in love
'Cause your mind is light
Your hands are free
You don't fear the results of your artist imagination
You live on a rainbow that's all your own
High above all, floating endlessly over the sun and into the clouds
'Cause you're no longer normal
You're in love
You're cursed with a disease that's hard to rid.
It makes life easier
You never have to concentrate on love, feelings and thoughts
Your drawing will just flow from your heart
To your hand onto your paper
At once you'll wonder where such
Art and Talent could come from
But don't say it out loud 'cause everyone
Will say that you're in love.
You beam at your work
You reflect on what started as clay and
Has been hand-molded into a vase.
This beautiful vase is you
All that is within you.


The sculpture is a result of your love.

# THE GIFT

At the remarkable moment when you realize
That this world is full of gifts

Your breath
Your physical body
Your spirit
Your love
Your heart
Your talents
Your mind
Your ability

But most of all your service to others

God sends blessings to who He can send blessings through
God gave His son—the most awesome gift of them all

Just consider how warm you feel
When you help someone with a bag or basket

Don't forget your emotions when you've helped a baby walked

Lest you be reminded the youth and math tutoring

Be mindful of the child and her spelling.
That smile after she spelled bicycle was priceless.

These gifts—priceless and unforgettable.

I remember when she read my favorite story to me at night over and over.

I remember when she taught me to ride my bike

I remember that she gave me a flower when I won the spelling bee.

But I remember most that when I needed her shoulder
She was there and held me tight for she knew that I needed that hug
She must've needed one too because she let go first

She picked me up when my mom was ill
And took me to have ice cream and to the movies

Gifts are to be handled with care with love and kindness.

They each have their rewards

Remember the gifts that you share with someone
May be the very thing they need to make it through to the next time

Don't take it for granted.

Give of yourself until it manifests itself into consistency

Give of yourself

Give.

Gifts.

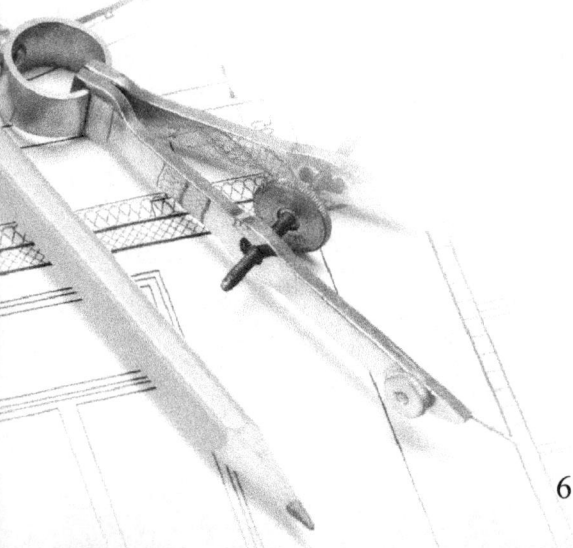

# REVOLUTIONARY

When he asked Nikki if that was counter—revolutionary, I thought of you.

I am now the educated Black woman by societal measures and
I must say it feels great

And although I flunked my MRS. Exam, my BS suits me better.
'Cause while I missed the MRS degree by a few points,
I earned my Ph.D. about me and my JD about life.

My focus is my new middle name so my priorities are back in place
And your insecurities are someone else's concern

Don't hate me 'cause I smile as I write
—He'll be here soon enough to capitalize
And exploit the love and passion and friendship

I bet he's looking right now wondering when
To make his approach
Besides I'm in no hurry
'Cause the Revolution took place within me

The revolution, it started an evolution

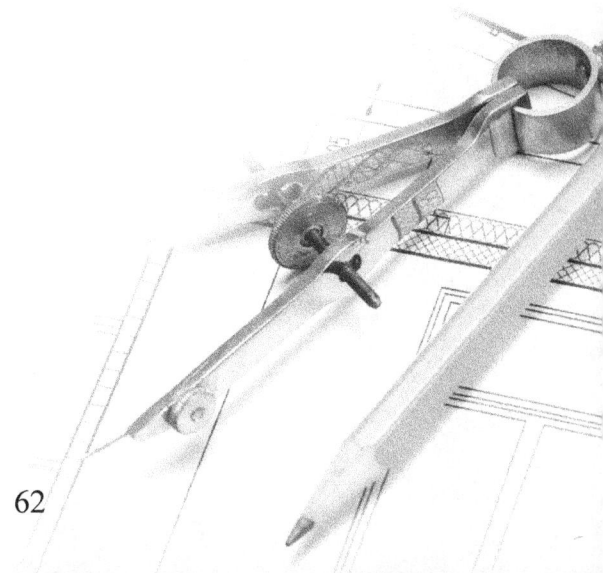

## DON'T KNOW ME

When I'm not around you don't wonder what I do
      Nor do you seem to care

How do you intend to discover the passion that
Eagerly waits to be provoked if you don't indulge
Yourself in me

You neglect to seek the inner strength and the passion
Struggling to surface—only wanting to be nurtured by you
And united with your soul
And matched with your passion
And coupled with your strength

See all you need to do is stroke my hair
And not let me be overdue for a
Body massage
And by the way, I need to moan and purr
Passionately in response to your touch and
Your warm breath on my toes
And at the nape of my neck.

The fact of the matter is that you don't know me at all

But that's because you don't want to know.

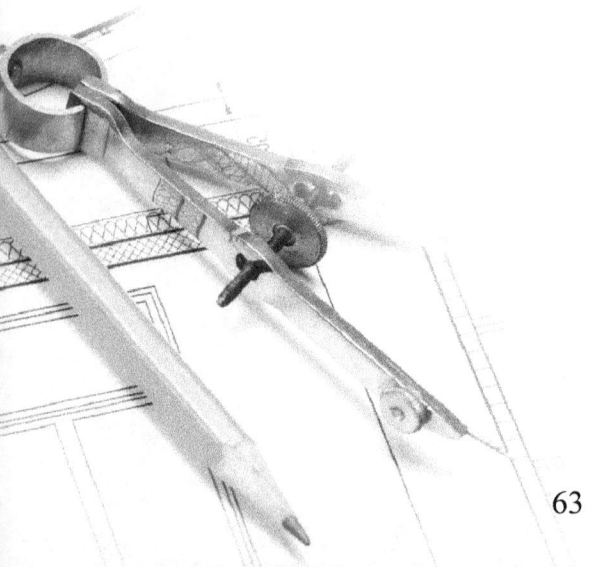

# THE BATTLE WITHIN

There's a battle that rages within
This battle of wit versus will
Wisdom versus naivete
Good versus evil
Peace versus chaos
        Controllable chaos even

There's a me that you don't know
Can't see
Can't feel
That me is dying to get out
But is well guarded
Shielded against the evil and pain of this world
Hidden even from you

The test is whether the surface me is manageable
Well no, probably not
Can you handle the me you see
'Cause the me that's on standby, is
Sensitive and can't handle hurt, is
Caring and won't handle rejection, is
Loving and doesn't sustain manipulation, is
Sharing and will crumble under closure, is
Dying to get out to love you

My soul yearns for peace
To leave or not to leave, the choice is yours
For to love her, the girl in the mirror
Created with God's very thoughts and with love

The battle that wages,
Rages within seeks a truce
Seeks a mate
Loves God and will not be
Doused with mere words but
Through active love.

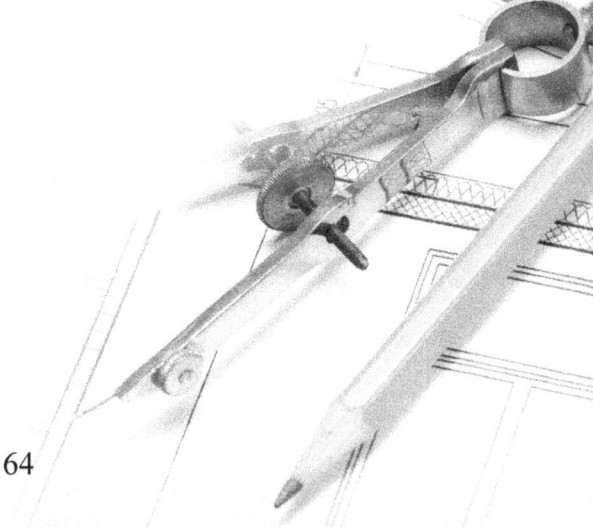

# HE STANDS IN YOU

When I called your name in need
And thought you looked away
It's Christ you sought
To meet our needs and
Heal our pains
To Him you turned to pray

So when you held my hand and
Cradled me at night
I wondered how
You stood so bold
Your fear disappeared
Old dismay turned bright

Then I know it was He
Who stands in you
The look on your face was clear
That when we love in His awesome care
When we unite as one
Even a amidst a storm
His love for us is reproduced
       And in abundance multiplied
He cares for us my dear
       As do you
So forgive me for not
Trusting your desire to help
Or your ability to make the call

He sent me you
That's sufficient
He stands in you
That's love.

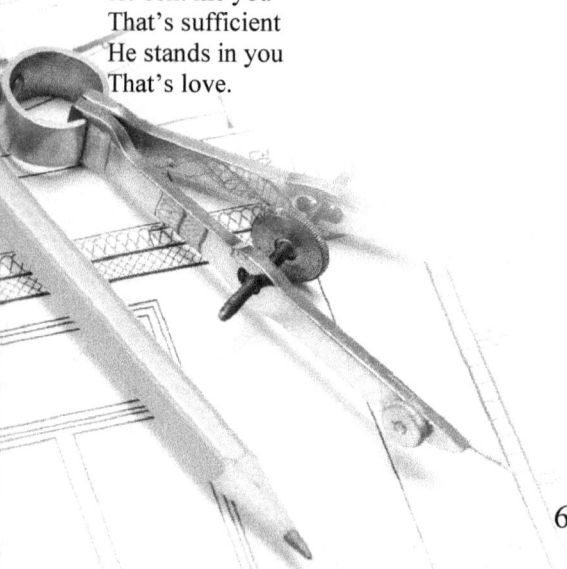

Onedia N. Gage

# ALL THAT I HAVE

If I offered you the box
Containing my life estate
Would you accept it?
Want it?

The box holding the essentials of my being,
I offer for you

Do you reject it?
        Dispose of it?

What is it that makes me trust you with
        The very crux of my soul and all that
        Led to its development?

My total being is in the box—
Everything I thought I couldn't live without

Please hold it—keep it

I present to you who I am in the confines of a box
A box I tried to live in and live without

This box not special at all
        Cardboard
        Brown
        Worn
        Used
        Taped
        Repaired

Detailing each crucial moment of my life
Often with a less than credible image

All that I have
I wish for you to keep
As a reminder of my life
And my misnomers, mistakes
        But mostly of my love

All the love I have.

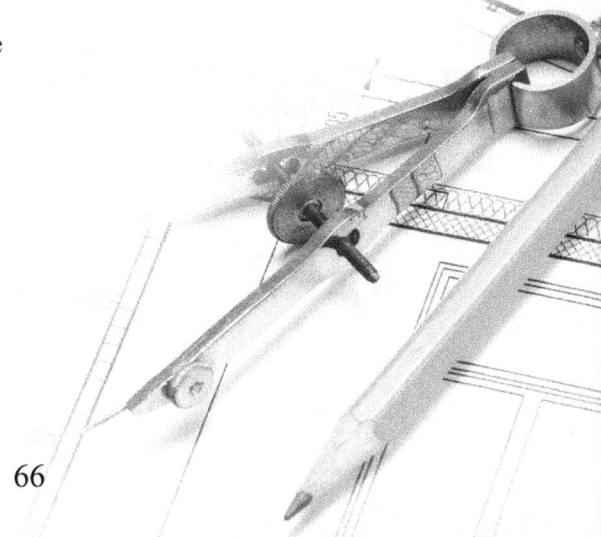

## **SHE**

Who is she that has your mind in flux
Who is she that has your soul's intentions captive audience

Who is she that holds the keys to your intimacy
So that there's no playtime for me

Special is a relative term
Composed of definition
Applied via perception

Where is my attention
And my affection

When do I get to look into the eyes and
See the things that I never hear from you

Oops, I forgot, just did
I looked up to see my reflection
Instead I saw an image of her

An image that revived memories of my self
My old self
The self that thrives on chaos
        While reveling in peace
The self that is consumed with passion
        While sharing compassion
The self that welcomes a challenge
        While appreciating the ease of accomplishment
The self that promotes spontaneity
        While planning the most detailed surprise

Have I lost the depth I once knew
Have I missed the growth I knew essential
Surely I stopped the self-improvement evaluations

Wait surely it's not an old image of me
        That has been left behind
I'm not that shallow

So, who is she?

Onedia N. Gage

# THE MAN IN FRONT OF YOU

What do you look like

How blind are we
That we don't see
That the person before your
Very eyes
Is wearing a disguise

Multidimensional
Lively
Character, he is

Wearing normal clothes
With casual attitudes

But behind those eyes
Is a surprise
For you and me

He's hurting and yearning
Confused and convicted

Hurting from brokeness
Brokeness from loss
Loss of love

Yearning for affection
Affection from a loving lover
Lacking passion

Confused about future
    Future of confusion
    Unsortable information:
        Success or failure—who decides
        Rich or poor—differing where
        Happy or sad—deepening the questions

Convicted by spirit
    Spiritual warfare amuck
    Warring for satisfaction
    Wavering in the face of adversity
Irrepairable damage
    Consumed with challenge
    Overwhelmed by conviction

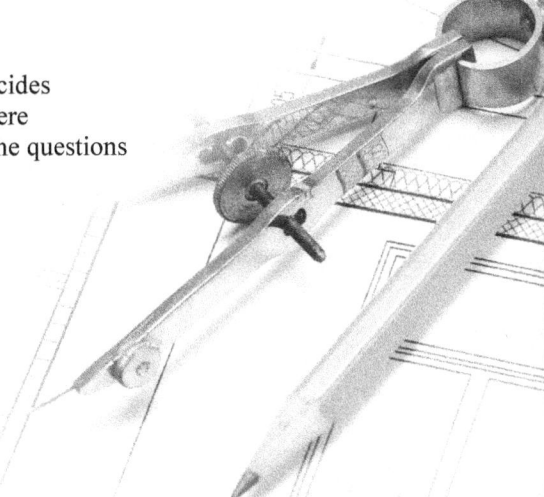

This disguise eludes and deceives
Perceived as elite, aggressive
Captivates
Stimulates
Motivates
Yet shy, demure, meek

Upon touching the face
The disguise slowly slides off
Slowly transforms into truth

Face the truth
The truth transcends
Transparency develops
Invokes intimacy

What do you look like
Blinders removed
Fort Knox loosened
Unsecured if you will

Transparent
Translucent
Clear

The man in front of you
You now can see
No more blindness
End fear

What do you look like

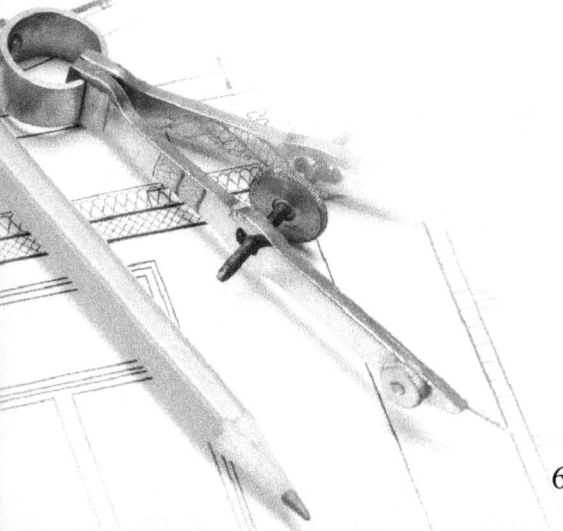

# WOUNDED

I wish I could be your healer
I wish I could be your comforter
Soothing your fears
Smoothing your scars
But this job calls for none other than God

Young brave warrior
You need healing
Your prayer warrior
Instinctively intercedes
For a stilling peace

A resounding, renewing and refreshing
Of your wounded spirit

Young warrior,
The redeemed of His church,
Blazing trails for His righteousness

Young warrior the
Omnipotent hands of healing
Are forthcoming
Submit to His hands

Your prayer warrior
Invokes the power of the presence
Of the Holy Spirit
The receptive spirit of the
Young warrior

True immersion in His word
His will
His way is the only
Way to achieve unity

Young warrior, reconcile your spirit
To the Trinity
For they bring peace, strength
The fruits of the spirit

God gives through people
Whose motives are pure
And whose rights are relinquished

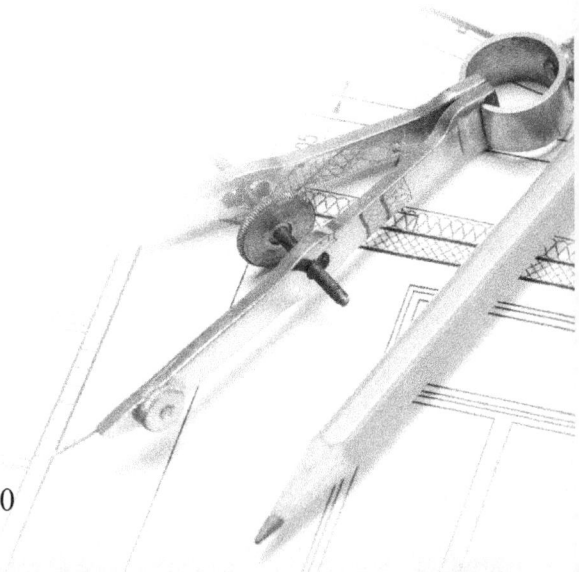

Warm warrior intertwine
Your spirit with that of the
Holy Spirit

Accept God for the soulmate He is

Be forever mindful that He commanded
Us to be still
Know that He is God and
Take refuge in His word

Seal your faith with prayer

My warrior
My mighty young warrior
Your prayer warrior is
Present and ever mindful of
Your needs

Wounded young warrior your
Prayer warrior intercedes.

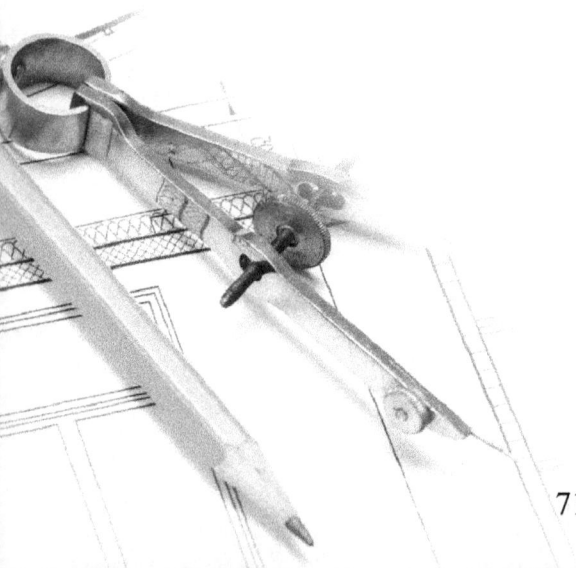

# SEARCH
## (On This Mission)

This destructive behavior
Is unbalancing my spirit

Wanting to find comfort
In the arms of a man

Not THE Man
But a man
A simple, powerless man
Rather than THE One
        Controlling life and its abundance

Seeking the human, fleshy being
        Whose decisions are made based
        On fact and emotion

Rather than the fulfilling, awesome power
Of the MAN
The MAN who saves, forgives and
Loves unconditionally

This rare love that seeks the truth
Because He knows the truth.
He is the truth.

No mere mortal can do near for you,
To you, or through you
What Christ can do

What in us seeks the real MAN
—the one who seeks us before we ourselves
—the one who forgives unconditionally
—the source of our strength
—the light for our otherwise darkened paths
—the source of our motivation
—the source of our inspiration
—this one who carries us when
        we are too weak to carry on

What in us loves HIM so,
Yet never enough

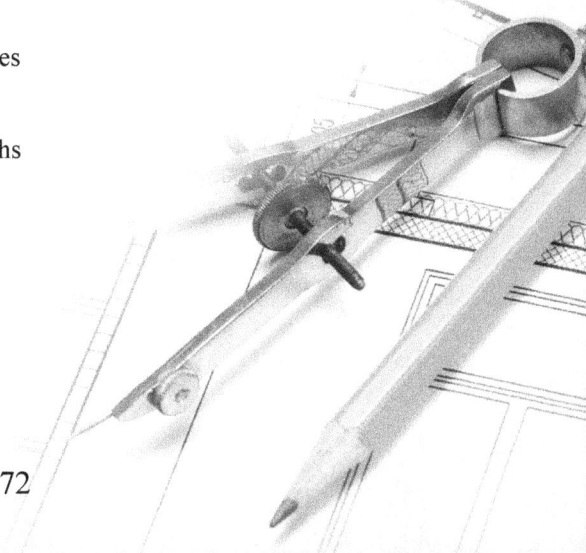

What in us seeks the wrong man

Especially when HE just asks us to stand

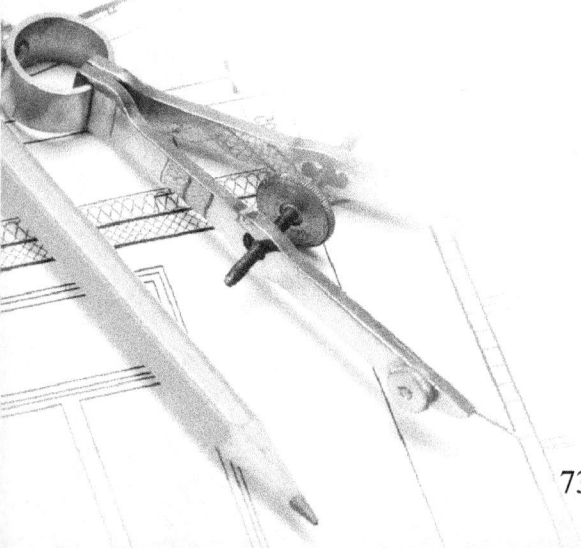

# EXPOSURE

You may never read this
Yet you know every word
Isn't that how most love letters start

I think of you
And pray
Pray for closure

As I pray for healing
Strength, yielding spirit
Ability to reveal, to invest

As I heal, I pray
I pray peace and faith
I pray for you

Thoughts of you as
I walked along the beach

Memories overwhelm
My conscious
Consumed my heart
Drowning the desire
Knowing your presence no more
Soothing reality
Reality—what a novel idea

Reality I didn't want before
Comfortability now

Blue salt water ignited a passion deep within
Strumming my heart strings
Stroking my soul's ego
Shining and burning into my mind's processes
Poised for intimacy

New, fresh, brilliant

Past gone
Present bleak
Future promising

Exposure to the newness of another
Comparable souls

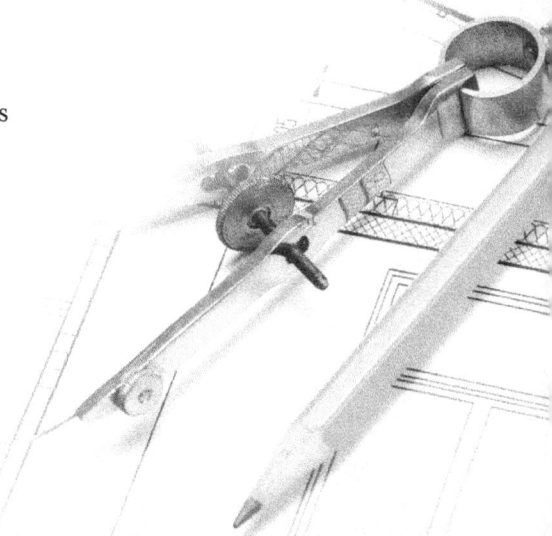

Intertwined spirits
United hearts
Intimate moments
Exposing my feelings to the uncertain

Exposing my heart to new hands
In new care
Exposure to dreams

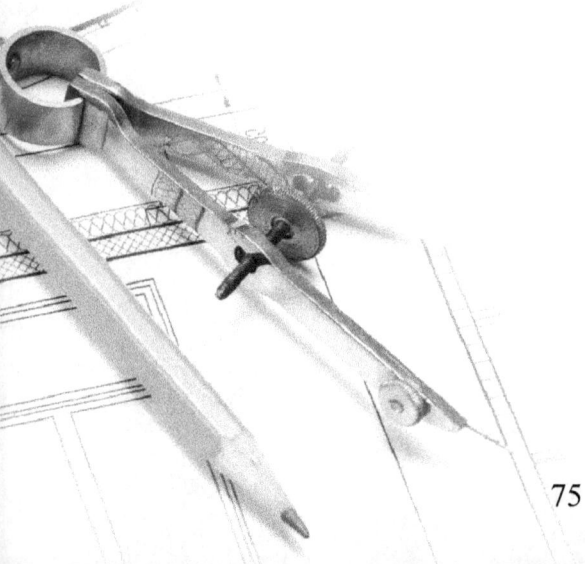

# RUNAWAY

Front of the city courthouse
Running for the life
The life of his own

Those black boys run away
For fear
For haste
For disgust

Black boys running
From the indelible justice
      Or the injustice
That perpetuates itself
Throughout society

Mere humans
Different expectations
Abnormal norms
Obscure standards

When will these boys be able to stop running
Running for justice
Running away from justice
Running for a life
Running for their lives
Stop running away
Start running
      . . . the chemical plants
      . . . the oil wells
      . . . the foundations
      . . . the boardrooms
      . . . the city
      . . . the county
      . . . the country
      . . . Our Homes

If I pray, then my black boys will overcome these obstacles and redirect that run.

# TEARS

When You turned my tears into heavy rains
When You transformed my pain into energy to serve Your people
Only You could move me in and out of the lives of others with few scars and blemishes
Only You could move into my thoughts removing my fears
Of course it was You that showed me that the silver lining inside the cloud
      Was inside of me all along
Yet it was platinum instead
Worth mistaken again
Obviously Your messages aren't clear enough
Or maybe not even to me
He was to kiss the tears away.

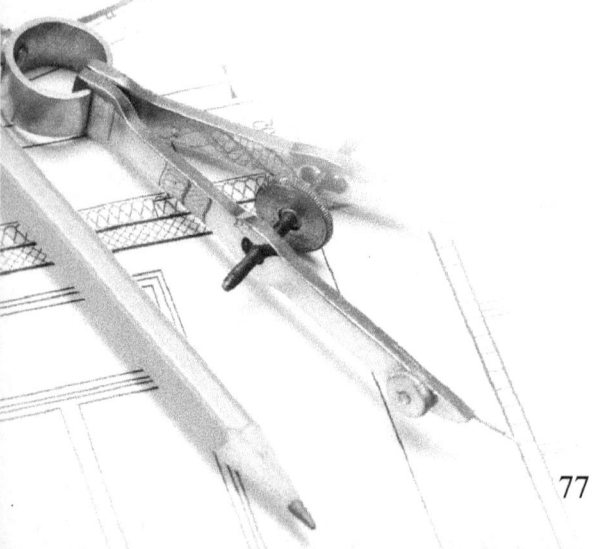

# DEFINING MOMENTS

In this life,
Defining moments don't come often
Yet sharing life with someone whom
God has sent is one such moment
Sharing life with each success, and
Failure, each triumph and disappointment'
Spiritual growth and spiritual warfare.
Sharing each defining moment.
I'm blessed to spend the rest of my
Definitive moments with you.

Love,
The Bride

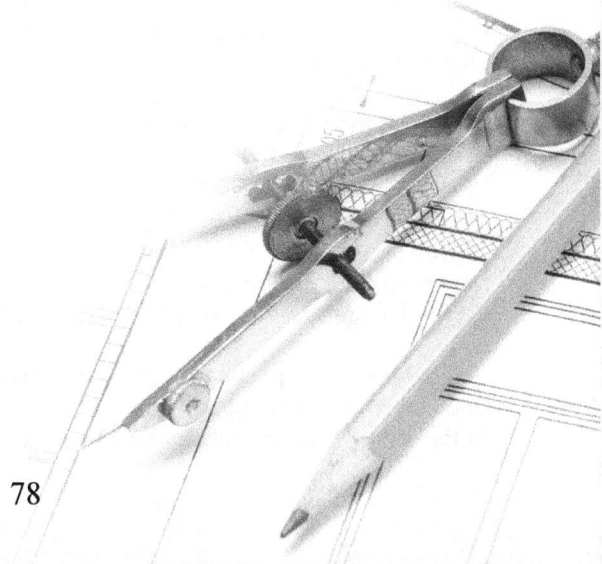

## THE TIE THAT BINDS

Celebrated your birthday this year
Moved by the prayer shared at the celebration:
      The tie that binds.

Four young men loved and cherished and disciplined to serve the Lord.
Woman, your absence has moved the life of a man that was operating with a hardened heart
      Now the clay is in the Potter's mold and His obedient servant
Troubles have come—Faith is waning
But that's on time for you and God
You have been there right at that brink , many brinks
The brink of disappointment

"Need you now"
      Loss of security—a waning faith
      Loss of love—a waning patience
      Loss of patience—a waning peace
      Loss of strength—a waning focus
      Loss of health—a waning purpose

"I miss you"
Nine voices, nine different heart—felt expressions
Nine prayers to God for this renewed stronghold on the heart, mind and soul

Touch our lives
Ask Him to hold us
God gives through people
Even those no longer of flesh

You've blessed my life
I wish to bless hers; 6 men and a little lady
That was you, too.

Imprint on the world—you've left several
God uses people to do His will
He uses you.

"Love you."
Nine hearts and many more.
Expressing their feelings about you and your impact.

God only sends prophetic wisdom to one who will appreciate its power
God moved you from labor to reward
At the end of your faithful service with results yet unseen, still

Oh Lord, My Lord, How excellent is thy name in all of the Earth.
Psalm 8:1

Lady, the brightest star shines for you through the love of my life and
I know that your spirit survives in each of them

The glue that binds that hearts and minds of men
Unyielding men

I need your blessings in my life
We know that you watch us.

We love and pray for you.

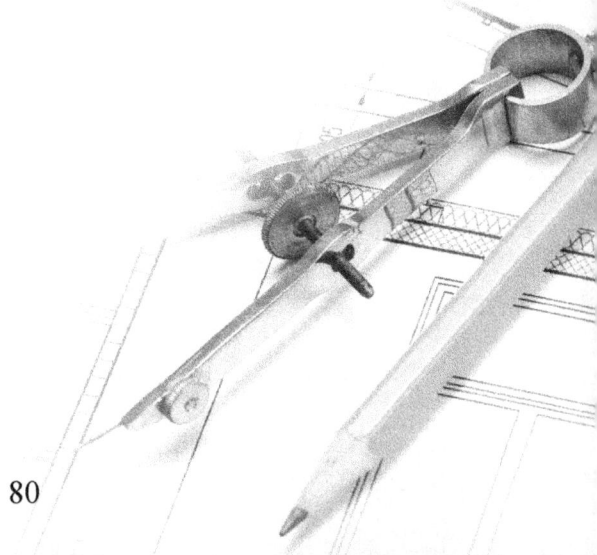

## LIFE AND ITS REWARDS

Appreciate life so that others may have it more abundantly
Share life so that the pitfalls of life aren't so burdensome
Love so that others feel it, see it and respect it

What you sow, so shall you reap

Life is real and so deep; so surreal, so tangible
Yet unseen

Sacrifice so that others may live

Limit your needs—diminish your wants

Allow the positive to dominate your spirit
Accentuate the positive within others
Search for the silver lining inside of those seemingly unending clouds
Remember that although at the end of the rainbow may not always be a pot of gold
	But the rainbow can stand alone and should be appreciated for that ability

Remember we need the rain so that we can grow
	Physically as well as emotionally

The length of time between the end of the rain and the beginning of the sun is your attitude

Life has its own rewards without our help.
We need each other
We need to love each other
We should fulfill each others wishes and dreams
We are all we have
Each of us one for the other.

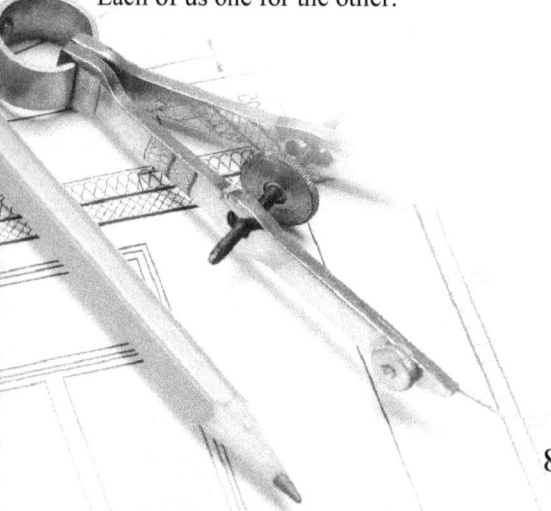

# DON'T WANT TO RUSH,
# DON'T WANT TO WAIT

Do I have a guilty feeling about loving you
Or is it fear?
Fear of failure
Fear of disappointment in you
In me
In us.

Faithfulness will never be questioned
Motives completely pure
Just love me fully, completely
I'll be right here

Five weeks, 2 days, eleven hours, 45 minutes
I choke so that the love words won't slip out
I stop just short of the questions
That it's too soon to know
We do the unspeakable, maybe even the unforgivable
But there's only regret because there's no ring
Is that so bad
He knows where my heart is
He knows what my prayers are

I shiver inside when you confess of missing me
I shake when your hands go through my hair

Though some feel unrealistic, I wish to be joined by the
Tenth month of the year

I need your spirit in my life

I want to love you as you deserve

"Woman ought to inspire man to do great things."

I want to do that for you.

I watch you sleep. At peace. One with our Lord and Master. Saviour and Prince.

I wish to be your helpmate. Your soulmate. Your best friend. Your lover. Your prayer and study partner.

This poem started with Don't want to rush, don't want to wait

The intensity that I feel for you
The request that I made and continue to make

I ask Him to send me someone that was of His word, with whom I could grow up and old. The father of my children. The head of my house. The triangular relationship. Two of God's children working toward loving Him. Loving each other as a result.

This man
In my life
At this point
At this time

Don't rush
Don't push
Wait
Wait for the Lord
Wait for the Lord to grant me the desires of my heart
      Through prayer and thanksgiving
Don't want to
Have to

Don't want to rush
Don't want to wait.

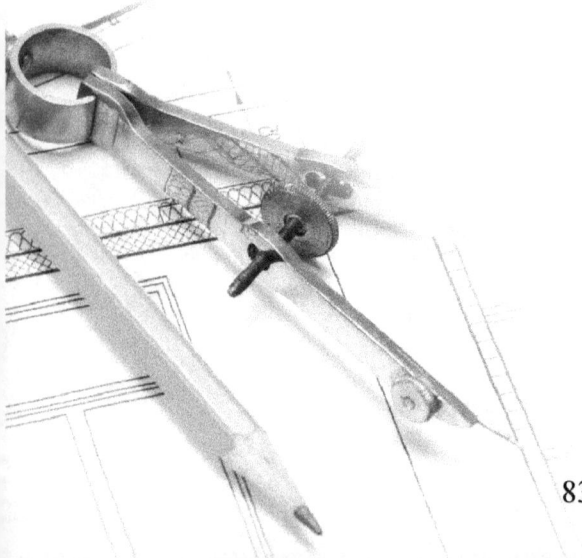

## NOT THE REVERSE

My facial expression gave it away
Shifting my weight from one leg to the other was probably
    The most explicit indication
That there was something wrong
"I hate cobblestone." I said aloud.
The shoe was next to a stockinged foot with a weak smile.
She looked down while I'm shifting from one to another
She grimaced slightly as she looked down at her own feet
The elevator stopped at her floor
"Have a better day."
Then she rolled her chair out of the car
I held my head low
Disappointed in my own selfishness
Insensitivity was never so obvious

Think before you speak.

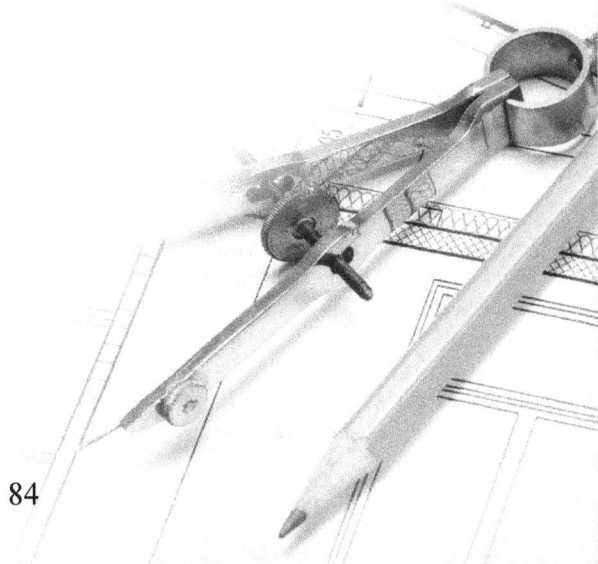

# THE BLUEPRINT

I'm special
I'm coy
Damsel in distress even but you would never know it
Private and Intimate
Intimately private
Privately intimate, even

I thought I gave you access
You listened to my poetry, my thoughts, my emotions
You saw those words on the page which I couldn't speak

You thought that the poem that Maya wrote was about
Someone else you knew but it was really about someone you know of . . . Me.

Pay close attention to my details.
You'll need that information

Maya explains:
      'Cause I walk like I've got oil wells pumping in my living room'
      'Cause I laugh like I've got gold mines diggin' in my own back yard'
      'That I dance like I've got diamonds at the meeting of my thighs?'

The stormy and strong persona, that armor that exists
When I'm in public and protected,
Protects the fears that I have within when I'm alone
Soothe that person, that woman that has little girl wishes and
Whom has been an adult since she was six.

Love her
Read her works
Play chess with her at dawn
Play the piano for her, even if you can't
Inspire her
Inspire her to cook
Rub her feet
Wash her hair

Realize that now that you have loved her
Her love is there for the lifetime.
For you.
Only You.

Need her as she needs you.
Love her as she loves you.

## MISSING YOU

If I told you I missed you
Would you really understand

I miss you encompasses the
Fact that yesterday I wished
For your warm, moist lips to be
Pressed against mine

I need you to know how much
Your absence effects me, however,
I miss you is too weak to
Describe such sentiments

Now I understand that there's
Nothing that you can do about
My missing you. There's nothing
I can do about missing you.

Sharing this all with you is very
Frightening . . . I have no idea
How you feel. What are you
Really suppose to do?

This comes at a bad time
This comes at a time when
I need to be held, kissed, loved
Cared for, massaged, caressed.

Now I know that this may
Come as a complete surprise to you
That I'm not satisfied, I'm not
Happy, that I'm lonely
I want a trustworthy companion

But I miss you is all that I can
Manage at this time
I miss you and wished that
I didn't yearn for you so.

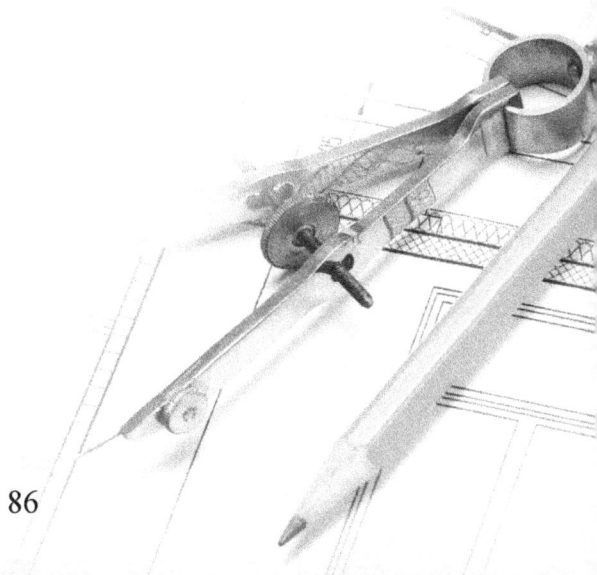

## ISSUES

I know that the list is long
But I'll give it right back
I'll give it back ten—fold
Those words of comfort.
Those passionate strokes
The intimate glances
You'll see your reflection through me
Don't worry
Regret will never surface
Peace will be standard
You'll love me without reservation, and unrelentlessly
Pause and recall what you love without regret
Then replace all those things with me.
I promise I won't disappoint
I am worthy of your love.

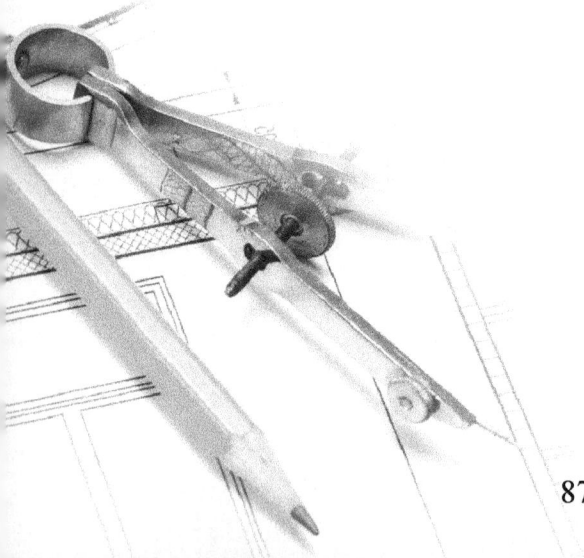

## POWER & DOMINION

Whisper to me as God on the patio
Blow the eloquent words of love as God moves
The tallest tree and the finest blade of grass

The heavens opened and encircled, engulfed, retreated—my
Heart went too

How far are you away from God?

Do you wish you could see the wind move?
    Or are you simply content that it moves
        Like blessings!


Move my life into a life where I experience Your love and
forgiveness and grace even when I'm not expecting any at all,
which is probably the most blessed.

Move within my life. Remind me of the beauty of
Your creations and that reminder only
Exponentially increases my appreciation
Of the Creator and His beauty.

My two favorite phrases have moved in meaning by ten—fold:
    "Oh Lord, Our Lord How excellent is thy name in all the Earth" and
    "God, Our Father afresh we thank you."

God,

    You moved the trees ever so swiftly them calmly, then not at all.
The birds chirped so pretty and the crickets reminded me of camp. The phone and the cars
Moved so that I could better hear the dog bark and the cat meow.
Now as for the bee that You showed us, well I was concerned. The grass is a
Remarkable example of Your power and dominion moving concrete, and consistent growth,
Not even humans could compose. The continue to believe that we can chose what motivates,
Moves and inspires us: Classic disobedience. At any rate, the planes and stars were the finale.
Beauty is not strong enough to describe the magnitude of light that is emitted from the stars that
Make up Your magnificent galaxy.

I Love you Lord.

## SMALL TALK

I called you at work to discuss the Dow
But I really wanted was to ask you to come over for dinner

I called you and discussed the weather
But I really wanted you to ask me to the movies

I stopped by your house to see your dog
But I really needed a hug, a warm one, only from you

I paged you to discuss business
But I really needed you voice to soothe my aches and pains

I saw you at the park playing basketball
And I really wanted to ask you to watch Sports' Center with you.

I talked to you after class about the seasons
But I really wanted you to read me a bedtime story

I met you at the youth workshop
But I really wanted your strong hands to rub away the tension from my body

I saw you at the concert and when you sent over the glass of wine
I really want to ask you to come over and rub my hair.

I make a bunch of reasons to call, or see you
But I really want you in our home on a daily basis
Because I care deeply for you and want you in my life

I just gotta get past the small talk.

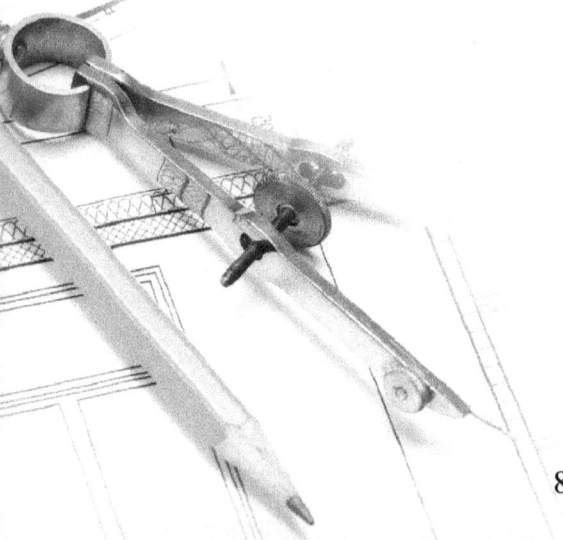

# ONENESS

Make no mistake
I love you
Your very essence captivates me
Your laughter reminds me of God's blessings
Your warmth of His love

When our eyes meet
I look beyond my reflection
To see your needs

"You complete me"

Make sure you know
That silver lining for which one searches
I have found in you

Sunshine, thunder, snow or all
I need you in my life

As my life shortens,
My appreciation for you grows

I remember when you first held my hand
Our first date

I recall when I first rested my eyes on your complexion
Wondering the content of our future
A future of defining moments
All with you

Our closeness
        Closeness that refutes all societal measures
Our oneness
        Oneness that escapes the mediocrity of any expectations
Our moments when we are breathless, motionless, indescribable

These simple words only culminate into
        My love for you is real and true

Our oneness overwhelms me
Overcomes my soul
Ignites my spirit

You make our oneness unique

Our oneness would be nothing
    . . . without you.

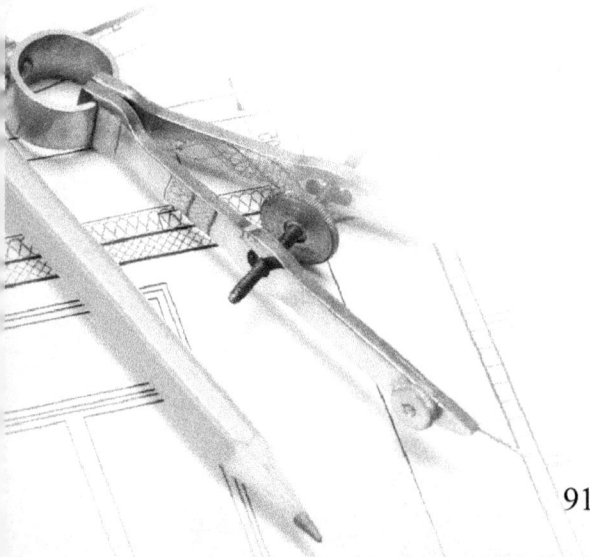

# DEAR ARCHITECT

Design specialist extraordinaire come quick
One of Your buildings needs You

Oh Architect, My Architect
Call him to You
He'll listen to Your call
Call him forward to serve Your excellence

What are You waiting for
Call him to seek You

Call him out
Beckon for him
Dear Molder, Builder, Constructor of many
Master of few

Show Yourself, O Great One!
Great One! Great One!

Am I the one?
Is it that he sees You through me?
Am I to lead him to You?

Dear Architect.

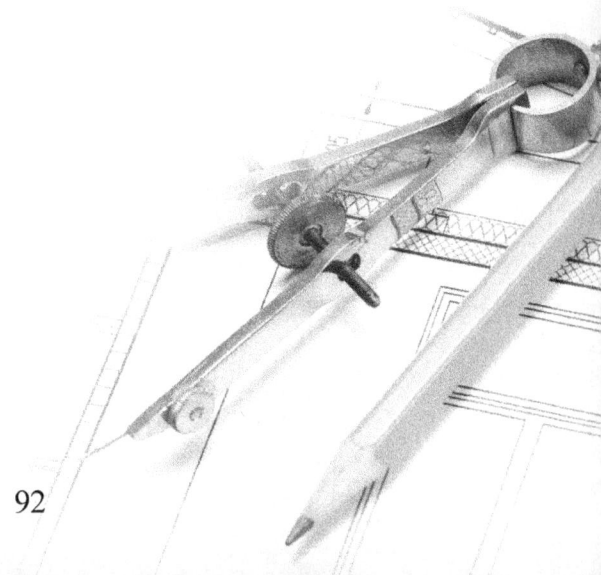

# MIDDLE

Middle too far?
Standing here waiting on arrival
Plane still yet to land
      —no e.t.a. at middle

Stretch, you say
Move, you say
Come hither, lovely mate move

Not inch
But boldly stride beyond the invisible mark
In quest for the invisible and
Moving target
. . . your heart

Meet me in the middle.

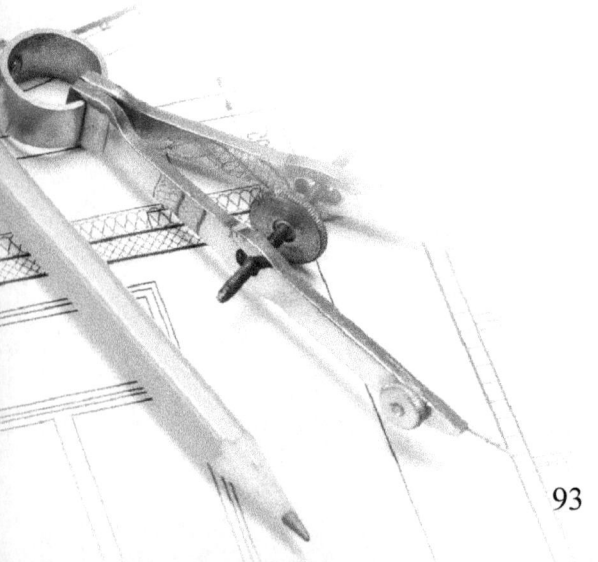

# ONE YEAR

And we made it
Some days I didn't think we could
Didn't think we would

**We** made it through
These days we can see the past
But these days were slow to come

**Made** it through though
Tough to see any day ahead
In this world without you

**Through** though hard
You would encourage each
If it were not you being missed

**One year** without you
Brought back memories of each year
With you

The love I remembered
Outweighed the loss
And certainly overshadowed
The tears I shed

Thank you for your wisdom and your love

One year
To grow to be who
You prayed for

By the way, my eyes ran
Across the words
"How has the world been treating you?"

My heart skipped a beat
My mind raced
My spirit prayed
My peace stilled my anxiety
My love flushed my face

One year
To realize that I only have
One day to love fully,

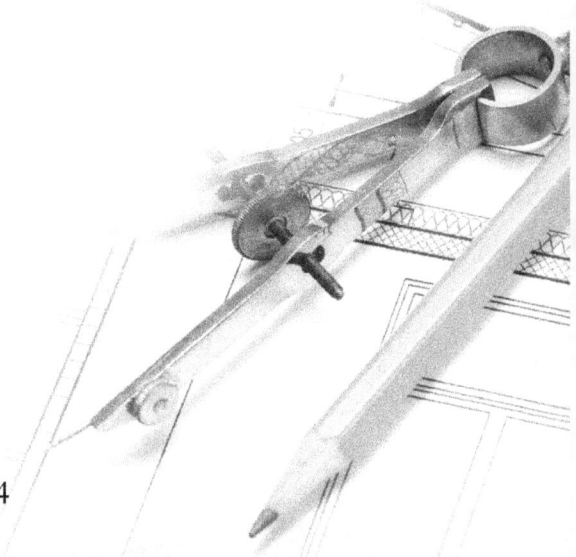

Unconditionally
As you loved us

One year
We made it through one year.

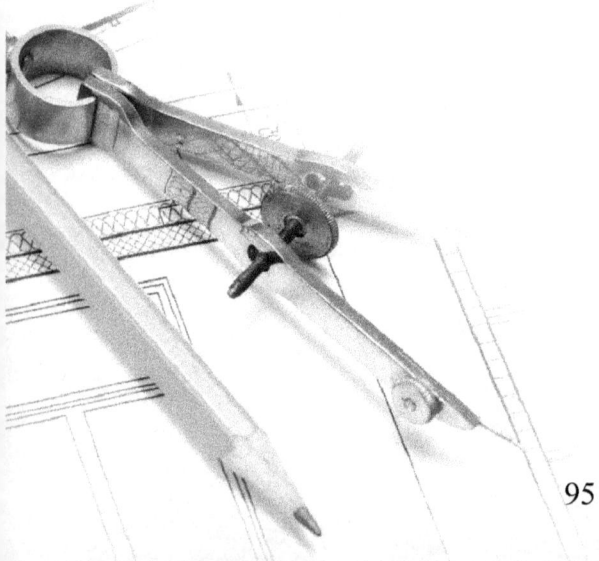

# ONE KISS

In just one kiss, she asked for forgiveness
He forgave
Relationship mended

In just a kiss
He vowed to spend each
Remaining moment of his
Life intertwined with hers

She agreed
They were joined

A simple kiss—
He said I care
I think of you

She said always
I wish for you

A delicate kiss
He confirmed his love
He matched her intensity

In a kiss
He spoke I love you
She replied forever, I love
They rendevous

This kiss
She invokes a passion extraordinaire
He responds with a desire unmatched
Love expressed stormy

One kiss
    So gentle
    So powerful
    So elusive
        Yet poignant

One kiss
    So profound
    So passionate

One kiss

Communicates love
Concern
Compassion
Strength

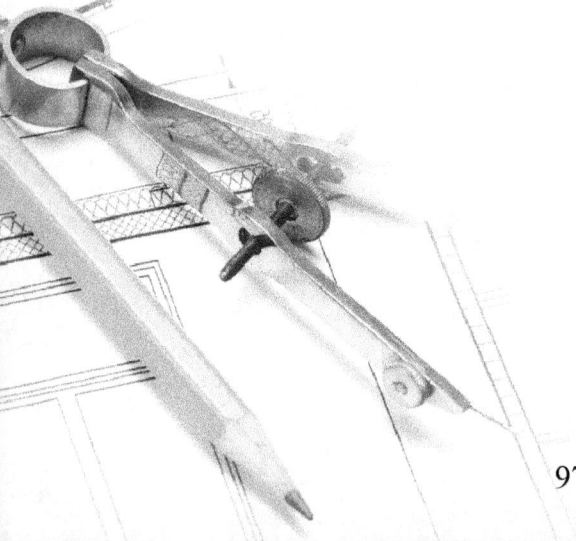

# THOSE DEEP EYES

Those deep eyes
Those deep, deep elusive brown eyes

Come over here, you
Sit those cinnamon thighs right here
I need to talk to you
I was thinking that those deep eyes
Needed some attention
I was wondering if I could love you
You know like the way you ask me to
When we first met

I just want to rub your hair
'Cause that relaxes you
And whisper in your ear
The things that make you tingle
On the inside

Those eyes call my name
Incessantly
Lovingly
Purposely
Acknowledging their power
Over my very being

Eyes yearning for my affection
My response to their request

Those natural eyes
Beyond which
Speak profound innocence
Intense passion
Mysterious peace

Naturally focused on me
Waiting for me to love
The person behind the eyes

Come over here
So I can love you the way
I've always wanted to
The way you ask me to
When we first met.

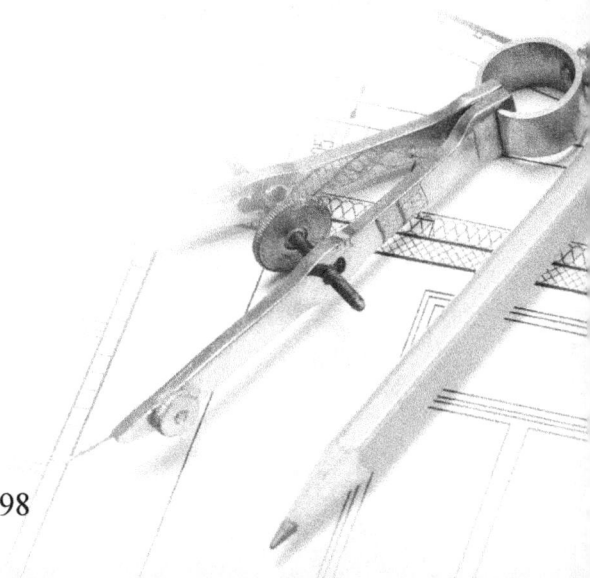

## WISHFUL THINKING

Walked to the strawberry patch
Far as my little eyes could see—
      Strawberries
Wished for you
Dreamed of a picnic
Imagined walking
Talking
Picking berries with you
Melted my heart

Wondered could we fall in love
Between the rows of berries
And the peach trees
Or would it be during
The lunch as I fed you
Freshly picked strawberries
And you drank champagne

There's a lake down the road
Maybe it was there you massaged my soul
While I walk barefoot along the side

Drove the countryside
Recalling all the day's events
Counting cows, shopping for property—
All while driving and thinking of you
Wishing I could be fishing at your side

Shopping for property where
We could make love in the lawn
Or on the balcony where the complete
Darkness of the night would cover us.

If only love was made of these same words.

# CAN YOU PROMISE ME?

(This promise means all to me.)

Long leisurely walks in the park,
        Along the beach
        On the strand
        On the Boulevard
        Swinging in the park
        Dancing 'til dawn

Fireworks
Carriage rides
Horseback riding
Fresh water fishing
Fresh strawberry picking

Play in the water
Bathe me in warm bubbles
Shower me
Wash my hair

Fly a kite
Play chess
Scuba diving
Biking
Hang Gliding
Hot air balloon ride

Listen to me
Talk to me
Read with me

Read my writings
Can we cook together?

Travel
Travel
Travel

Can you promise me all these things
Still love me
Hug me
Hold me
Passionately
And openly

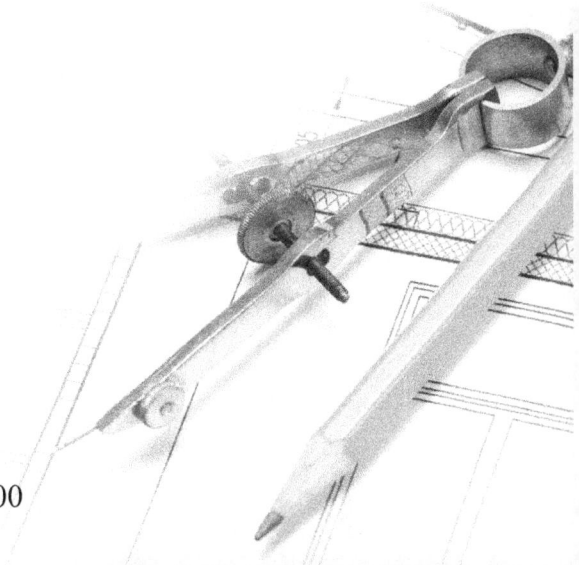

And often

Can you relate to my mystery
My mystique
My abstinence
Can you deal?
I wouldn't make you promise if it weren't important.

Can You Promise?

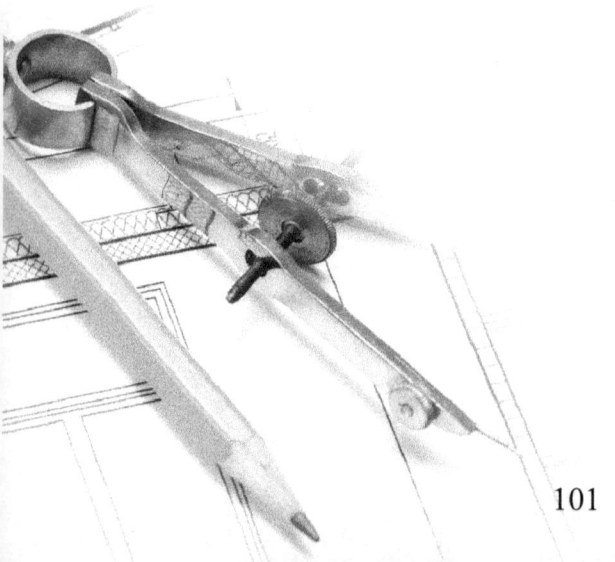

## NEVER SATISFIED

Isn't one woman enough
Why this endless pursuit of me?

Doesn't she do enough to show
        Her undying love?
She cares for your kids
But you claim she doesn't talk

Doesn't she seek to meet your
        Every need?
She sends your mother presents
But you complain she doesn't listen

Hasn't she been there through
        Each valley?
She worked two jobs while you were in grad school
But you repeat she's tired when you crawl into bed
        Sometimes well after midnight

Hard to comprehend
Your logic
Harder still to understand
Your confusion

Isn't she enough
Isn't she all that you ask for
Isn't she all you need

Your dark times equal a million midnights minus her support

But you never think of that, do you?

The nerve, the gall,
        The audacity—the blatant disrespect
She is at home washing your clothes
Making your meals

. . . And you are here talking to me
Asking me out as if you were single

Never satisfied.

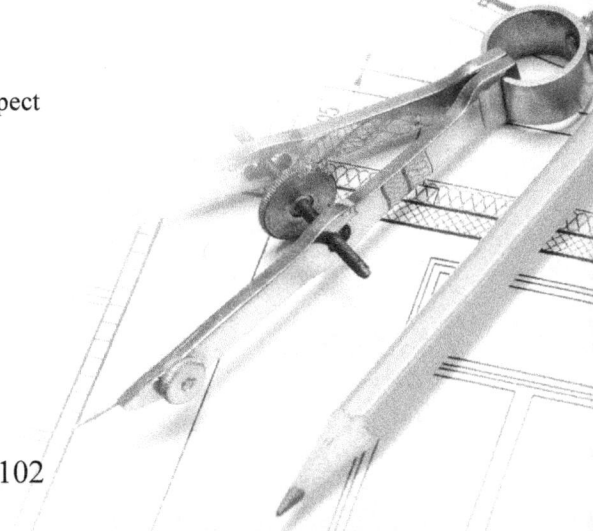

# A DAD'S LOVE

If I sit in your seat
Then I would remember the countless times
That you talked me through my tears
About
      Life
      Work
      Love

If I curl up on your chair
Then I may forget that you are no longer
Present to reassure me or diminish my fears

I sit next to your chair remembering the days
Where we would talk and watch television
Play Dr. Mario
But more importantly than that the
Communication when we didn't speak one word
Now I understand it all

Thank you for being the dad I never really had
Thank you for loving my mother unconditionally

Thank you for your wisdom
For your love
For being truthful and concerned

Thank you for my mirror
For storing the dress under your bed

Thank you for your prayers
Need you
Miss you
Love you

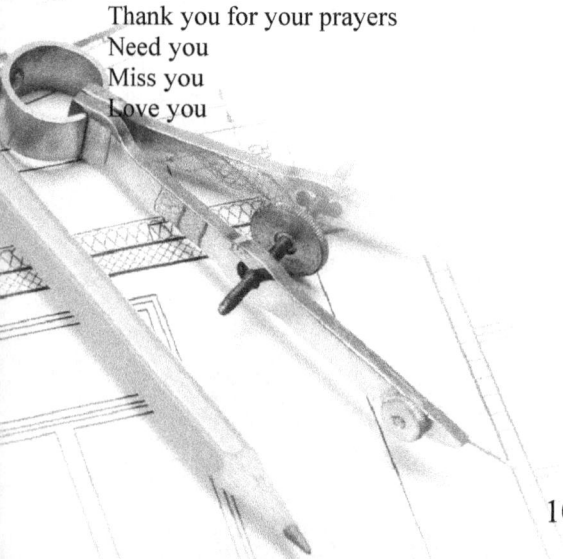

# THE HANDKERCHIEF

Tears of turmoil
Tears of triumph
How many tears have you
Washed from that handkerchief
The handkerchief that would say
If it spoke
I dry each tear
Each tear that falls to her blouse
Each tear that crosses the bridge
To the eyelashes
But I told her that these
Tears are not for her
I remind her that each
Tear demands a testimony
Someone watching needs to see those tears
They need to see the shedding
Of the bondage of the storm
Tears evident of storm-stirring
Testimony is evidence of storm-shedding
The handkerchief shared that the
Tears are all different
She carries emotions inside which
She never shares
I stay by her side all night while
She dabs her face to catch the falling tears
One day she gave me away
To someone who had her same hurt
Then I became her testimony
She shared my comforting ability
She cries
God heals
I comfort
She shares her testimony
She tells of how I've blessed
Those tears are gone
New ones come
But she grows by passing me on.

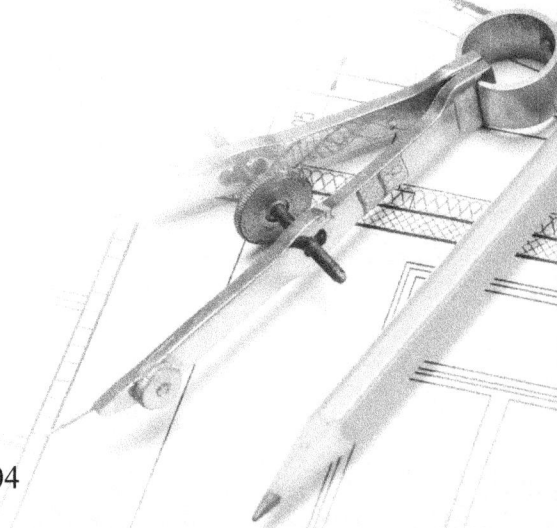

## THE PRICE YOU'VE PAID

As you carry the weight
And the plentiful burdens
God moved you out of
Your self-pitying
Broken-spirit
Bowed body

You hesitated
All you knew were mom, dad
Husband
But with God and me
God moved
God moved you beyond your fear
To His faith

Faith you have not confessed in eons
Faith you denied
Faith you discovered

God honored you to a faith that
Literally saved your life
As you sacrifice as Christ did
For this world
Carrying the weight

You came to Christ after
Your intercessors
You were already saved when
Your prayer warrior interecedes
God provided all of our needs
Even some of the wants

Remember San Antonio, Dallas, and Galveston

When you said yes to God's
Love and obedience
He answered abundantly
Bountifully
Beyond your greatest imagination.

## THE CIRCLE OF LOVE

The armor you wear cannot even protect your heart
No shield covers your soul
Both open and vulnerable to the outside

Spirit
Emotion
Care
Love
Faith
Hope, even, perseveres the ugly
> The unjust
> > The unforgiving
As well as the unforgiven

Returning to the heart without protection
Is it really unprotected
How vulnerable is it?
If we examine the facts
The heart has a few defense mechanisms
The little hate
The subtle fear
The slight insecurity

They exist
They exist to counteract the myth
Of the lack of protection
They never totally overcome it though
They never totally compensate for the heart and soul
The heart and soul still needs love and attention and affection
They both need a care-giver
The same care-giver
The nurturer
The blood is on the end of your sword
The sunshine is on the end of your sword
The healing power is in your hand which is
Wrapped around the handle of the sword

Your love grows love
Your care breeds care
Your protection fosters the growth which
Leads to love then
Lends to care
For the hand around the sword
Replacing the armor around that heart and soul

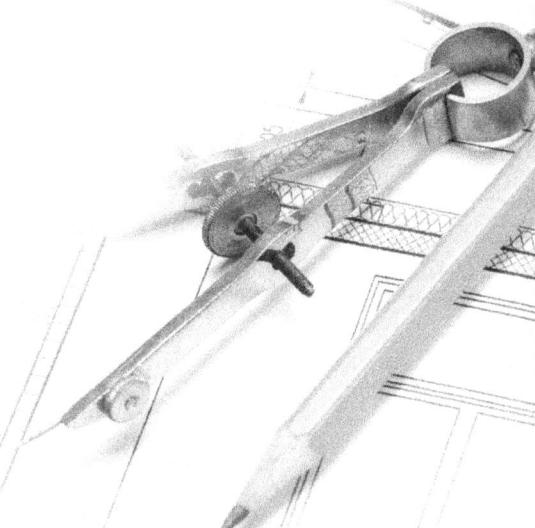

# PERFECT WORLD

In a perfect world
There would be no speed limit
There would be no law

(This imperfect world presents the challenges)
In a perfect world
People would say please, thanks, excuse
Of course, no anger, no pain

In a perfect world,
No war, no hunger, no disease
True democracy exists

In a perfect world
There would be love
Lovers would be true
Love would be real
In a perfect world
There would be no tears
There would be no fear

In a perfect world
You would be mine.

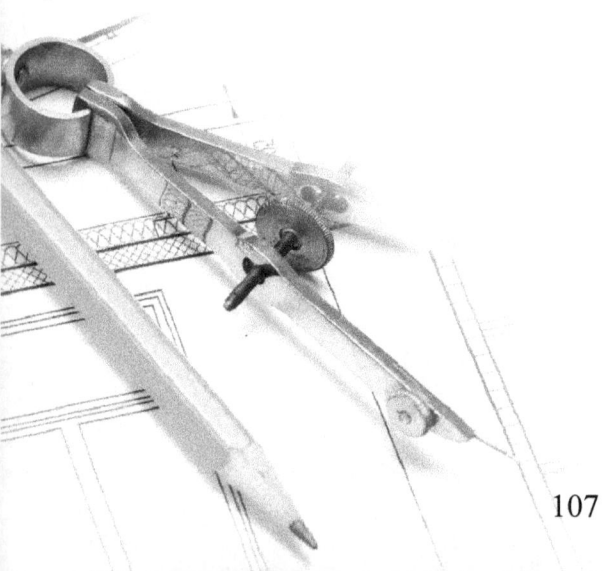

## **AS ONE**

How bold you are to capture
My heart
My soul
My spirit
All without my consent

How bold are you to decide that enough
Love existed between us to share
      . . . forever
That our separate existence needed
To be made one

How bold you are to discriminately
Develop a life long plan
Include my being
With love and care

How bold of you to invade my thoughts
Only to displace my fears
Replacing my singular status
With a plural disposition

How bold you are to broach
Love with such fervor
And no fear
Such completeness
And no reservations

Your boldness
My consent
Your persistence
My commitment
Your perseverance
My dream

Our Wholeness
Our Love
As One

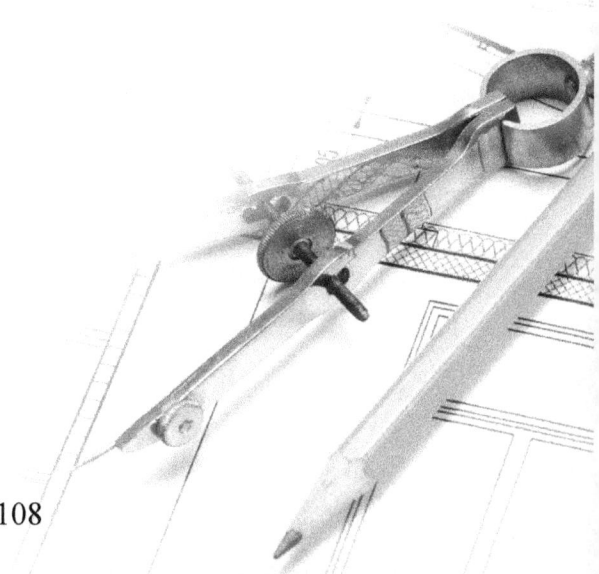

## **FOR THIS LIFETIME**

For hearing my thoughts
Understanding my dreams
And being my very best friend
For filling my life with music
And loving me without end
              . . . I do.

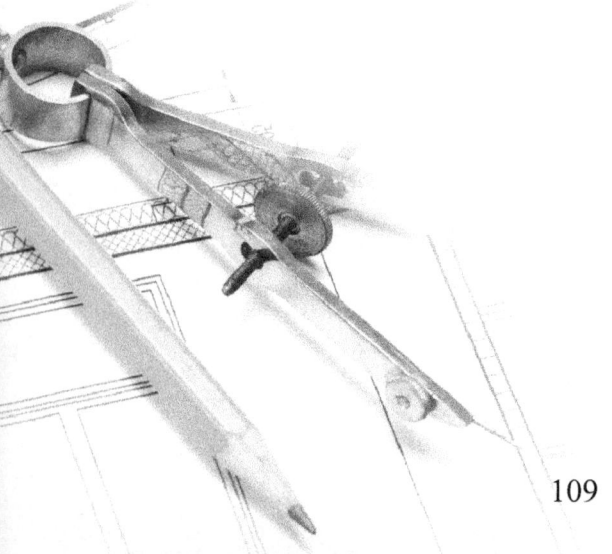

## RAIN DROP DREAMS

The drips and drops
Made me think
Of you
Today allday

The drizzle made me
Wonder what I do
To make you happy

The thunder kept me
Guessing why
You love me so

So I ask myself today
Allday
How have we made
Our love last

But mostly I dreamed
Dreamy dreams about
You
And your whispers of love
In my ear
At night
At sunrise
Of your love for me
That made all the difference

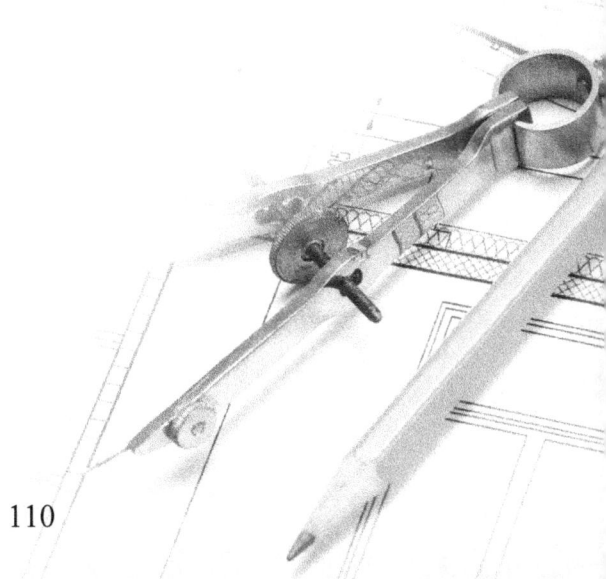

## LOVE'S LEADERSHIP

Gentle
Inspiring
Soft warm tender kiss

A kiss that spoke desire
Begged attention

He drew me in—closer
Closer than I intended

All with one kiss

He captured my heart—fully

He led me through his kiss
Into the leadership his manhood offered
Then to the love he desperately
Desired to share
There he embraced me
There he held me
There he kissed me

I let me him lead me
Through his kiss.

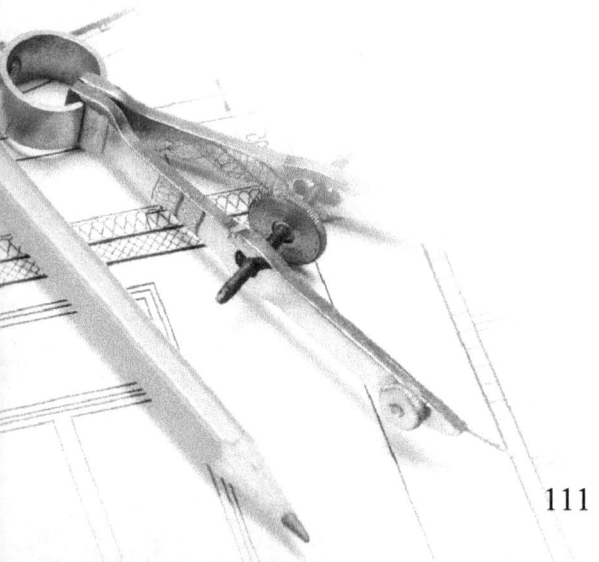

# ARTIST'S EYES

The eyes of an artist

What makes you see what I don't?

What makes you hear what I can't?

What makes you feel what I won't?

Different makes difference in the eyes of an artist

Expression-filled
Pure
Influenced by outside
Motivated by inside

In an artist's eyesight
Lies the answers to
The unanswerable
To the unspoken
To the unreachable

Unreachable souls
Needing love
Support
Encouragement
Peace

Teachable spirit

All in an artist's eyes.

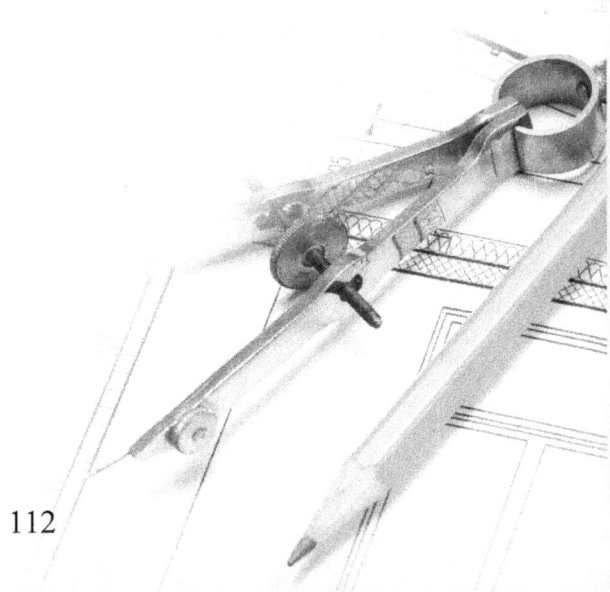

# PERFECT WORDS

Finding the words escape me
Perfect ones impossible
Words meaning too much
Yet not quite enough
To describe the unthinkable
The indescribable

Imagine what words evolve
Describing the soul's depth
Love's adventures
Sadness
Life's desires
Dreams deferred
Fear

If only I could master the
Perfect words
Describing my soul's depth
My heart's matters
My mind's thoughts

Then and only when will you
Hear the perfect words
For which I seek to speak

If I could be true to you about my feelings

And truer still about my words
Would I draw you closer
Or move you from my person
Completely

The difficulty lies in finding the
      Perfect Words.

## MILES OF FLOWERS

Pink and white flowers
Brought one home
To get the name
It died

Bluebonnets
Seasonal
Protected

They were the view
For some two hundred miles
As I thought of you

A background of strong sax
Bespoke the tone for
Intense thoughts of you

Missing you started the moment
I left your presence

Missing the looks that make
My insides tingle and twitch

Missing the rub of your nose
Across mine

Missing the feel of your touch
On my ear as I wake

Missing your hand in my hair
As I drift into dreams of you
    . . . of us

Missing your warm embrace
Missing our tender kisses
Which translates into all the love
Residing in your heart

My thoughts forced me to
Uncover the name of the pink and white flowers

They answer to love.

Love Flowers

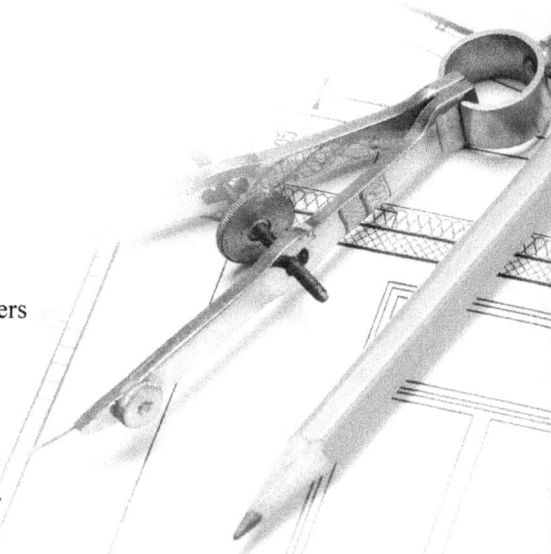

## VENUS & MARS

Venus and Mars not at all that far apart
Imagination key
Imagine a massage
Sensual and relaxing
Refreshing and renewing
Imagine a lover as thoughtful as you
More even
Completing each other's sentences

Think of your glee
If the love of your life
Respected your pet peeve

Lovers compatible
Loving constant
Love complete

The differences between Venus and Mars
Distinguishable by commonalties
Mystery defined during intimacy

Venus and Mars closer than most
Not really too far away
Imagine moving closer to Venus
Imagine moving closer to Mars
Imagine Venus and Mars in love

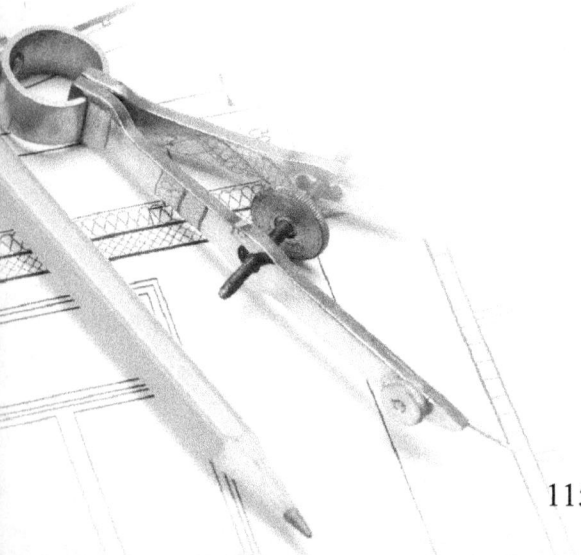

# SILLY

Ms. Williams wrote a song about it
      Want to hear it. . .

'Cause I was silly enough to believe
That my commitment to God would
Impress you into respect
Respect for me and my lifestyle

Silly was I to believe that you would still
Befriend me after announcing the
Life I lead

Silly of me to not know that my abstinence would
Cause your absence

Silly of me to dream that you could obey the
Commandments of the One who created
You, too

Silly of you to force me to choose between
God's love and your desires

Silly of me to invest my feelings in you
Believing they would be returned

My desire to love you is as
Silly as this poem

Having expectations of you were as
Silly as this verse

Silly am I still to believe that I
Sought your approval for
My Ordained Lifestyle

Sillier still was the time I spent
Debating my worthiness
Determined to provide proof

Awesome is His Glory
Better yet His deliverance
Of me to Him
Worthy
Unharmed

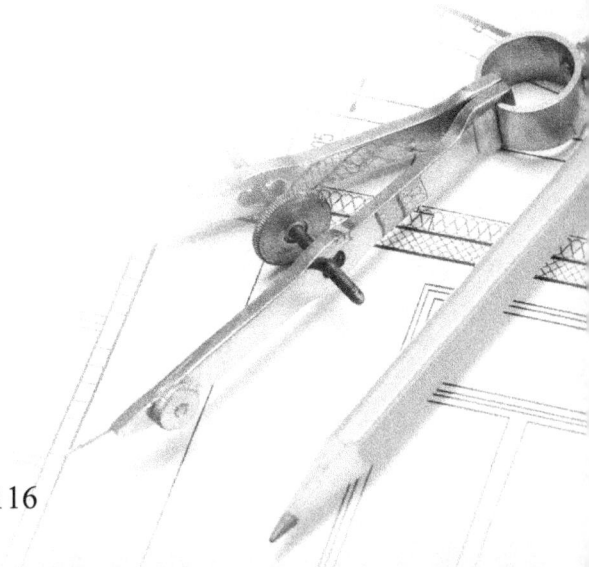

Unsacrificed

Silly was me wanting you to meet my
Needs when you don't meet your own

Silly too was hoping, dreaming
That you were the one, when
He already had a plan

Silly is putting a square peg in a round hole
Silly was demanding that you
Fit into my life
My way
My timing

Silly was issuing authority in my life
To a creation rather than
The Creator
While questioning Him

Goodbye, Silly.

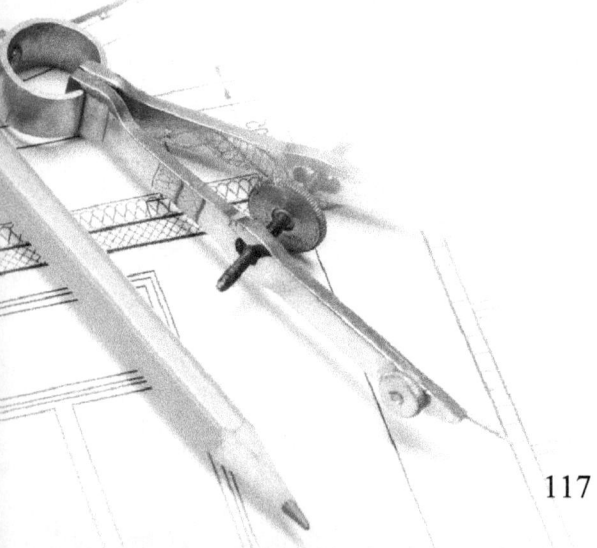

## SHE WALKS

She solves the world's issues
    In a walk

She simply trods until
    Life's pomp and stance becomes easy

She walks life's burdens
    Into submission

She walks as an example of life's
    Incomplete sentences and
    Less than grammatically correct expressions

The ease of her stride tells of her journey
    Of her perseverance
    Of her pursuit

The challenge of her steps are transferred
    From her spirit

She walks to salvage her spirit
    Sometimes barren and broken
    Hidden behind the ample armor
    Disguised by the humble outfit

She feels his love and His embrace
    Cradle her

She hastens her pace
    Longer, longer walks
    Closer, closer intimacy
    Intense, intense walks
    Clearer, clearer vision

She frees her spirit
    Through a stroll

She walks into
    Renewal
    Revival
    Refreshing

Her journey
Her destiny

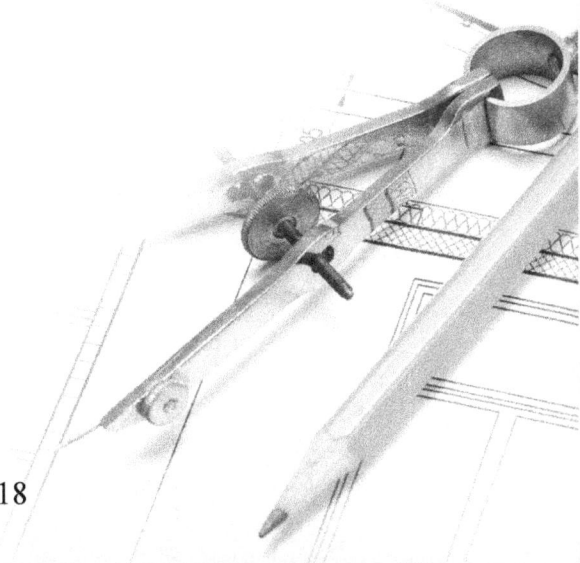

His plan
His love
        Demands her walk

She walks.

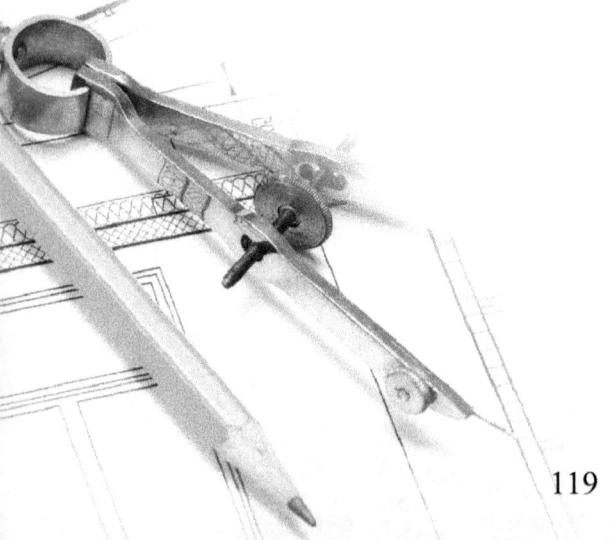

# IN RETROSPECT

Saw that movie we saw on one of our dates
Imagine that
Actually I just saw the end
It was different without you
Why was that?
Same movie
Same me
Was it that important?
Your presence, I mean
Didn't seem important at the time—then
But now as I wander
I wonder what could've come
What should've been
What happened to compromise?
Conversation?
My retrospect always misleads me
I must stay with my first mind
Oh well, who cares
I wasn't supposed to get nostalgic about
Some silly movie anyway

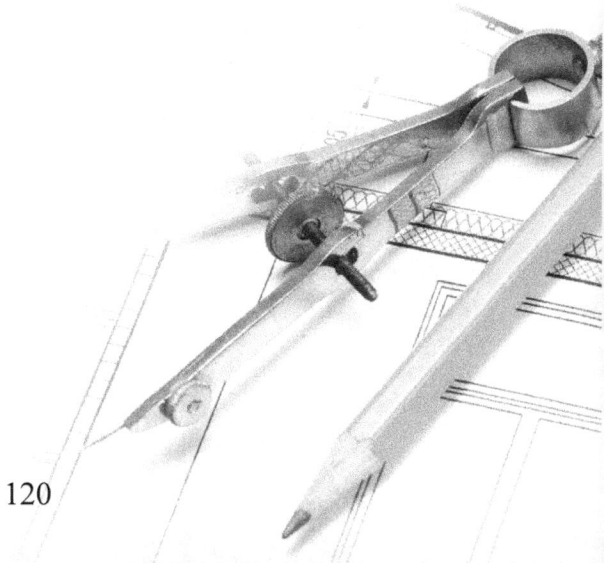

## THE GLUE

If I have you then
Maybe he'll love me
Perhaps when you come
Things will be different
He will see my point of view

I'm banking on you to be the
Glue for this relationship
And although wrong
I'm just hoping that you will
Keep us together

I realized that there is something
Missing from this relationship
I think you are just what we need
To regain focus
Regain stability
Create momentum, even

He's got to love me more after
You are born
He has to want to stay
He has to want me more
He won't leave now

I just want the love that
I know he possesses
He won't show me
Why?
Why is that?
Why is that he can't show me the
Love I know he possesses?

But that's about to end
You are almost here
When I rub my stomach
When I read to you
When I talk to you
It's out of love
Love for you
Love for him

I love you baby
Thank you for being our glue.

# DREAMED

I dreamed of you before you loved me
    Dreamed of your smile
    Dreamed of your voice
    Dreamed of your scent
Awoke restless in anticipation of your presence

I missed you before I knew you
    Missed our walks
    Missed our drives
    Missed our pillow talks
    Missed your hugs
Yet I searched for you

I asked for you a million times
    Asked for your arms
    Asked for your partnership
    Asked for your passion
Make no mistake
I almost fell for several substitutes
More than I want to count
Thinking that they were the answer
Glad I was wrong

I practiced being the me for you
    Perfect to meet your needs in just the right way
    Practiced being the wife of your dreams

I prepared to build a marriage overflowing with love
    Prepared to love so passionately
        So strongly
    Prepared for intimate glances across an ever so
        Crowded room reminding you that my
        Love is real
My love for you is everlasting

I dreamed of our lifetime together
I dreamed of our love together

I dreamed of you

When He sent you, I was ready
Ready for our lifetime

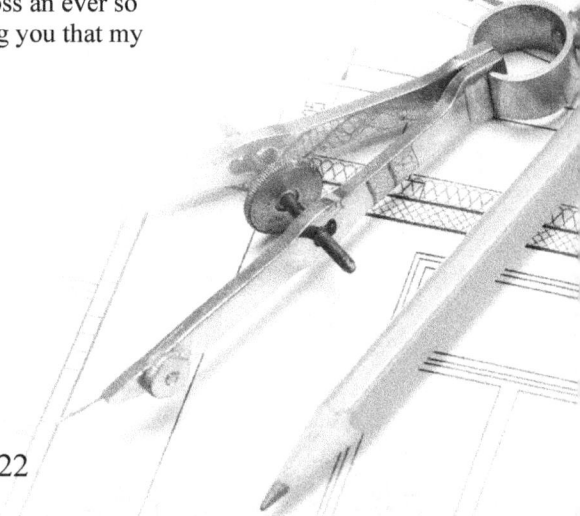

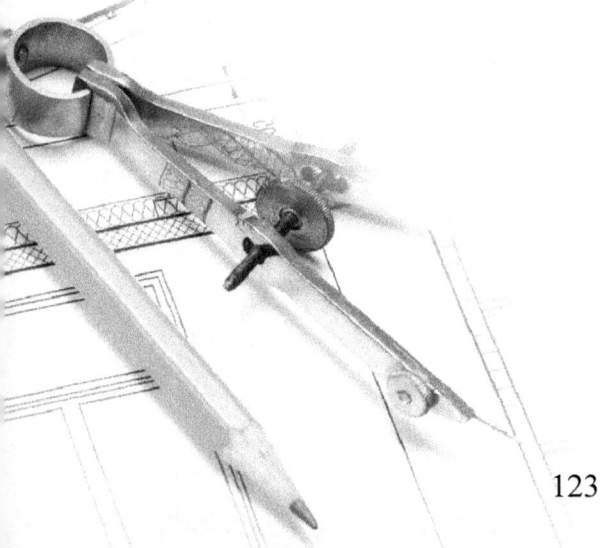

Onedia N. Gage

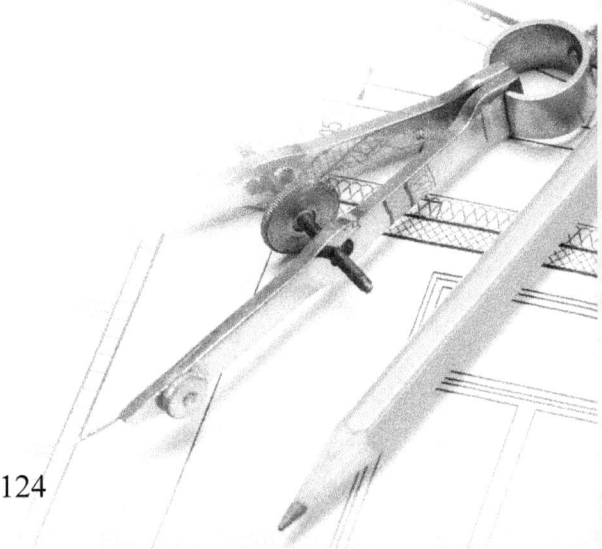

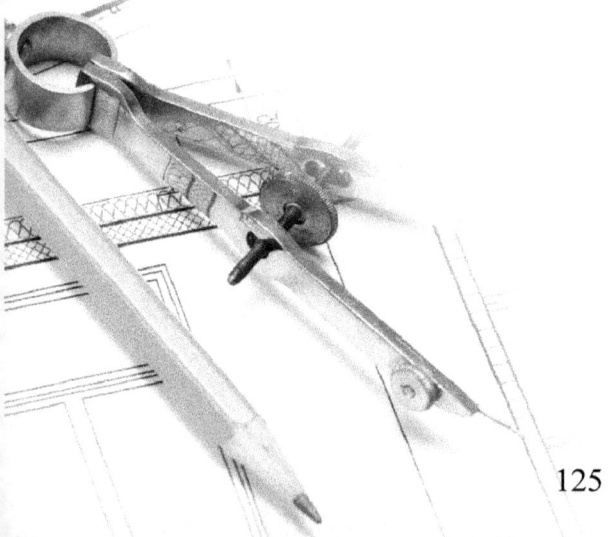

## ABOUT THE AUTHOR

Minister Onedia N. Gage has been writing since age 13. She has written through each of her storms and her sunshine. The gift of writing is ever present in her life. She is often seen with a pad and pen. Rev. Gage is truly transparent in her writings and seeks to share her testimony with others. She hopes others are inspired and decide to share their story with those of us who need to hear it.

**As We Grow Together Daily Devotional for Expectant Couples** addresses Christian parenting. There is an accompanying **As We Grow Together Prayer Journal for Expectant Couples**.

**The Blue Print**, poetry that exposes her innermost thoughts, was developed over 15 years. She encourages the creativity in others and is starting a writing circle for those who write. She desires to turn what has previously been a hobby into full-time career.

**In Purple Ink: Poetry for the Spirit** captures the essence of the journey through pain and a reconciliation to God. The road away from pain is a complicated one so she offers this work to insure that you are not alone and certainly not forgotten.

**The Measure of a Woman: The Details of Her Soul** discloses the secrets and the nuances and the idiosyncrasies of a woman. **Measure** is bold and states clearly that we are more than conquerors and the journey of a woman will certainly show her worth.

**On This Journey Daily Devotional for Young People** covers issues young people struggle with daily. Because there is a shortage of resources which exist for the sole purpose of assisting our young people with biblical sources for worldly situations, Rev. Gage designed **OTJ** for that purpose. **On This Journey Prayer Journal for Young People** offers young people the opportunity to journal their prayers and concerns in a format comfortable for them.

She authored **Promises, Promises**, a novel, out a need for female heroines of her time.

Her life philosophy is three – fold: A) "What have you done today to invest in your future?" B) Reading is essential to your positive contribution to our community; and, C) "If not me, who? If not now, when?" She feels her time is best spent when youth benefit from her experiences.

Because of her commitment to youth and community, she facilitates youth enrichment workshops. She believes that while exposure to certain things is common in other cultures, in the African American community, it is a special occasion. She uses these opportunities to encourage our youth to succeed. Other workshops she teaches "Nobel Woman Stand," "New Year, New You," "Choosing God's Best," and "If Not Me, Who? If Not Now, When?" In addition, she facilitates Vacation Bible Schools, retreats and lock-ins, specific to communication and group dynamics for young people and women.

She created Purple Ink, Incorporated, to serve as publishing and promotional company for her writing and public speaking. Recently, Purple Ink established a foundation to provide funding for youth educational organizations and battered women's shelters.

Minister Gage answered her calling as a minister in October, 2003, and was licensed June, 2009. She is an active member of The Church Without Walls where she is on the clergy team, the women's ministry, has served with children's ministry and Vacation Bible School.

Because of her volunteerism with the Houston Area Urban League's NULITES, she was elected one of the youngest board members of the Houston Area Urban League. She is also a member of YMCA Board of Directors, Spaulding of Children-Houston Board of Directors, Zeta Phi Beta Sorority, Inc., National Council of Negro Women, Toastmasters, International, Top Ladies of Distinction, and "Sistah to Sistah," a literary review group.

Onedia N. Gage is a native Houstonian. She is a graduate of Kaplan University with a Masters in Business Administration, Lamar University with a Masters in Education in Education Administration, and University of Houston, central campus, with a Bachelor's of Science degree in Economics and a minor in African American Studies. She is a graduate of Bellaire Senior High School. She is currently pursuing her Ph. D. in Business Leadership and Masters of Arts in Christian Education.

She is has two beautiful children.

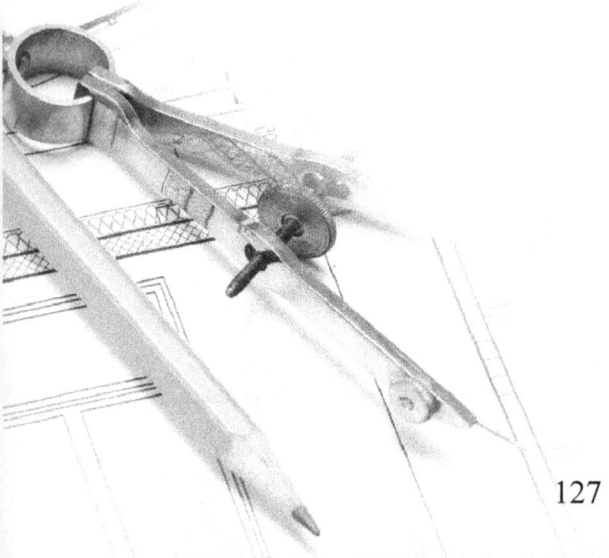

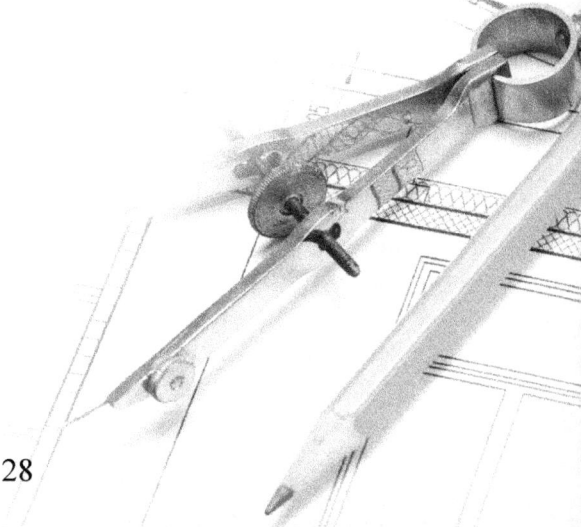

www.ingramcontent.com/pod-product-compliance
Lightning Source LLC
Chambersburg PA
CBHW032054150426

43194CB00006B/523